Praise for Jennife{r}
Financial Planning for Global Living

"Having suffered the trials and tribulations of going expat in my mid-career in the 1990s, I wish that I had been given the information in this book those many years ago. Jennifer Patterson takes a complex and emotional subject and lays out a clear strategy for any individual or family trying to navigate the many conflicting forces at play when you move country, move job, and move out of a safe "home" environment. Jennifer lays out a bold manifesto, based on solid principles and experience. This book can save you money, your marriage/partnership, and a lot of emotional turmoil that normally leads to ill-health. Well worth reading and acting on the key ideas."

— Lorne Mitchell,
Managing Director, Objective Designers Ltd.

"Although this may be the financial planning profession's best resource on cross-border planning issues faced by people navigating among a variety of national and local tax jurisdictions, Financial Planning for Global Living also serves as a valuable guidebook for how to live a better, more prosperous, more intentional life."

— Bob Veres,
Publisher, Inside Information

"Jennifer Patterson is passionate about the importance of creating a financial foundation that supports individuals and families living globally. This book is the culmination of her many years' experience — both personal and professional — of the realities of cross-border living, and it resonates with the warmth and wisdom she brings to this often neglected part of our lives. She blends practical guidance with a firsthand understanding of the challenges cross-border families face, helping us to achieve long-term security in an ever changing world. "

— Rachel Yates,
Creator, The Expat Lifeline

"Jennifer Patterson has written a must-read primer for anyone amidst or considering cross-cultural living... Read this book — and learn from one of the best. Financial Planning for Global Living is the exhaustive field guide that should be included with every international assignment so the issues that matter are dealt with from the start of this wonderful global adventure."

— Andrew Jernigan,
Expat Insurance Broker and Co-founder,
International Care

"A must-read for anyone considering a globally mobile life, Financial Planning for Global Living provides practical tools to overcome the paralyzing fear of uncertainty to help us move our lives forward. Jennifer Patterson shows us the way to plan for a cross-border life with enough flexibility to adapt to an ever faster changing and unpredictable future, and to the complex constraints of conflicting local laws. Her process allows for both long-term flexibility and short-term focus, never losing sight of what is important: Today, right now, we can design and live a personally fulfilling life on our own terms, consistent with our core values and personal aspirations that recognizes the importance of our human capital as a key component of our wealth. Enjoy!"

— Marina Hernandez EA, CFP®,
MHtax

FINANCIAL PLANNING FOR GLOBAL LIVING

Go Beyond Cross-Border Tax and Legal Complexity to Location Independence, Financial Freedom and True Life Satisfaction

Jennifer A. Patterson, CFP®, CIMA®, TEP

This publication contains the author's opinions and is designed to provide accurate and authoritative information. It is sold with the understanding that the author and publisher are not engaged in rendering legal, accounting, investment planning or other professional advice. The reader should seek the services of a qualified professional for such advice; the author and publisher cannot be held responsible for any loss incurred as a result of specific investment or planning decisions made or not made by the reader.

The information contained in this book is not intended to be "written advice concerning one or more federal tax matters" subject to the requirements of section 10.37(a)(2) of Treasury Department Circular 230 as the content of this document is issued for general informational purposes only.

The information contained herein is of a general nature and based on authorities that are subject to change.

Tax law is continually changing. This book reflects U.S. income tax law as it applies to taxable years ending on or before December 31, 2017, and is current as of November 30, 2017. At the time of this publication, the U.S. Congress had taken up consideration of significant revisions to the tax law that could have an impact on your tax obligations and the way your taxes are calculated in tax year 2018. Any reference to H.R. 1, originally known as the Tax Cuts and Jobs Act, should be considered preliminary guidance, based on analysis and understanding at the time. Further guidance by Treasury, regulations or future technical revisions are expected. Even more than usual, applicability of the information to specific situations should be determined through consultation with your tax adviser.

CFP®, CERTIFIED FINANCIAL PLANNER®, and are certification marks owned in the U.S. by Certified Financial Planner Board of Standards Inc. (CFP Board) and outside the U.S. by Financial Planning Standards Board Ltd. (FPSB). CFP Board and FPSB permit qualified individuals to use these marks to indicate that they have met CFP Board and/or FPSB initial and ongoing certification requirements.

ISBN: 9780999257913

Library of Congress Control Number: 2018935522

Printed in the United States of America

Life + Wealth Achievement Plan and Cross-Border Life + Wealth Achievement Plan are brands powered by Life+Wealth Achievement Formula™

The Life & Wealth Compass and 8 The Facets of Daily Living are adapted from the "Wheel of Life" Copyright ©, Money Quotient, Inc. Adapted and used by permission of Money Quotient, Inc.

DEDICATION

I want to dedicate *Financial Planning for Global Living* to my clients, who, over the years, have shared their concerns, ideals, secrets, fears, failures and hopes for the future with me and allowed me the privilege of working with them. Without you, my work and subsequently my life would have less meaning.

And to my financial planning friends and colleagues from around the world for their collective and individual wisdom. Specifically, Brian, Dale, Devang, Terry, Raoul, and Rob: I am grateful for our early work as the Cross-Border Planning Alliance. We can be proud of the fact that a search for "cross-border financial planning" brings up so many new names. To Marcia, from the early days at the broker-dealer through the last ten years at Patterson Partners, thank you for listening to my ideas, helping to filter them and assisting with carrying out the ones that survived. And, more recently, to David for also listening and filtering, but more importantly for carrying the torch into the future.

Also, to my husband, Jeff, without whom my cross-border journey would not have happened. We've discovered, firsthand, the many challenges and unique features of cross-cultural marriage by simply going through life together over the last twenty-five plus years. Although we've had our highs and lows, the journey is one I would not have wanted to take with anyone else.

And thank you, Curtis and Megan for being your unique selves, as your dad and I tripped through the weaving of three cultures into our family traditions and way of being, and for turning into such strong but caring multinational, multicultural, young adults. I look forward to seeing your contributions to our global village.

CONTENTS

FOREWORD

I did not know what I did not know, until I met Jennifer Patterson.

I have served as an officer for the world's largest retailer, worked in fifty-three countries, dealt with nine-figure P&Ls, built and sold numerous entrepreneurial ventures, and worked with coaching clients around the world. I assumed my financial savvy was more than enough to meet my goals.

I could not have been more mistaken. I now realize that my corporate and entrepreneurial experiences, coupled with investment and financial planning advice born out of the 1920s, are not adequate in today's globally mobile marketplace.

When I met Jennifer I was instantly intrigued and impressed by her wisdom, experience, and responsibly maverick approach in challenging the financial planning stalwarts I had heard previously. She had all the normal industry designations (CFP®, CIMA®, TEP) and the résumé of an industry veteran, but I could immediately tell something was different about her.

While attending an entrepreneur's mastermind event in the Caribbean, I paused briefly in a lush tropical courtyard just off the lobby to say, "hello." Two and a half hours later, I stood in the elevator stunned at the financial concepts and options that I did not know nor thought existed, much less were available to me. I quickly realized that I was not well equipped to build the lifestyle I want today and the legacy I want to leave.

As a fifty-year old entrepreneur with a desire to continue building my business for some seasons to come I have a vast vision and numerous ideas of how my wife and family want to live in the months and years ahead. We have multiple business interests, friends and clients around the world, and a growing passion for sailing with a lifestyle that matches our globally mobile business.

One would think that an observant ear, consumed with gleaning your true goals and dreams, would be the norm for the top-tier financial advisor world. Sadly, my family's interest in cross-border living was loosely considered, as other teams dusted off rote plans and stale approaches, proving their inability to understand what is most important to us.

What Jennifer really showed me were options.

In *Financial Planning for Global Living,* Jennifer arms her readers with the information and questions to build the portfolio that will perform for them today, as well as far into the future, whether they are U.S.-based, Mediterraneans in-residence, or tucked away at anchor in a turquoise water adorned inlet in the Caribbean.

The fact that I do not have to make those decisions yet – as we continue to invest – is genuinely liberating and exponentially calming.

It makes complete sense (now) that I seek out a visionary financial planning team that understands a global economy that is more intimately linked by the millisecond. Why would I even consider investment models that had not taken into account the Internet, blockchain and the globally mobile business owner?

With the introduction of the *Cross-Border Life + Wealth Achievement Plan* and the *5As* outlined in *Financial Planning for Global Living,* my wife and I found instant clarity and focus that allowed us to understand the cause and effect of life decisions today and in the future. And when paired with our desire for options we can continue to build and invest from a significantly higher and infinitely better-informed place.

I wholeheartedly invite you to be enlightened and challenged by *Financial Planning for Global Living* and encourage you to seek Jennifer Patterson's expertise. You will not be disappointed.

People often ask me, "What is the path?"

Financial Planning for Global Living is the path. You are holding the roadmap in your hands. There are a million outside forces that can wreck your efforts. All are just distractions. Choose the process you believe in most and focus all your efforts on that process. When you do — your goals come to you.

Learn.

Take action.

Enjoy the journey.

— Kevin Breeding
Entrepreneurial Mentor, Coach, and Speaker

Dearly beloved
We are gathered here today
To get through this thing called life.
— Prince

WHAT IS FINANCIAL PLANNING FOR GLOBAL LIVING?

As we approach the 21st century, we are witnessing a dramatic shift in the context of our relationships, how we work, and our lifestyles. Today it's easier than ever to work remotely, to make money online serving a global client base as a coach, as a consultant, or as tutors. Tennis pros and even dog trainers can now teach a global client base. These days, technological and digital advances have given us a global reach and more time, more freedom and more options for a globally mobile lifestyle.

But trying to be successful financially and have successful personal lives today while using the skills and processes developed for traditional lives lived in a single country simply doesn't work.

Most of us didn't have role models to provide the kind of financial or personal guidance we need in our new globally mobile age. Our life and wealth training came from watching our parents, who may have been skilled in the old model but not in the new one.

Today, we think differently, we live differently, we work differently, and we want options not restrictions. These days, we can live, work, play and make a difference *anywhere in the world*, not just because our employer offers it but because we want to. In our global village we can have financial success *and* stronger relationships. Our personal and financial lives have transitioned from a traditional one into a global one yet we don't have the tools to fully grasp all the options available to us or to understand how to avoid the myriad pitfalls that can endanger our finances and even our relationships as we cross borders.

In *Financial Planning for Global Living* you'll learn the model and the methodology that will give you confidence—whether you're relocating, straddling borders, facing repatriation or considering entering the global village—to not only find the destination of your journey but to create the financial map that will get you there so you and your family can live a full, financially secure, happy and well-structured life—across borders.

This book is for you if...

Financial Planning for Global Living is written for a myriad of readers in a multitude of situations.

It will help you achieve that next level of financial success, joy and fulfillment in your life no matter where you are now—even if your life is well structured and you have total clarity about who you are and where you want to go in life. Even if you know how your current assignment or business structure, skills, and current country of residence fit into the larger picture of your personal and professional life—you will find information and clarity within these pages that will benefit you and your family.

Financial Planning for Global Living will also guide you, if:

- You're in transition and you're uncertain of what the next phase is and because of this you're hesitant about planning for the future.

- You're overseas, having worked through at least one cross-border relocation process, or you've been asked to consider a specific role overseas.

- As the "accompanying partner", you've put your career on hold to raise your family and it's time for you to get back to sharing your skills and talents with the world.

- You're considering the impact of cross-border living on your career or business, your relationship and your financial situation.

- You're a national of two (or more) countries. You may have figured out that your life is "cross-border" by default rather than by choice and you find yourself with a lot of opportunity as well as complexity.

- You're an entrepreneur who wants to, or already works, globally but you and your financial structure are legally limited to one country and you're ready for the next level.

Many of us are satisfied with where we are today but we rarely look to the future to consider the next level. For instance: how to improve key areas of our life such as our well being, social and interpersonal relationships, our career, or financial health.

Maybe you're considering how to take steps to leave a legacy for your children or how to structure your day-to-day activities to positively impact your future. If goals like these are important to you, have you considered what you would need to do, or *stop* doing, to obtain them? Or what would you need to develop—personally, emotionally, strategically or financially to accomplish them?

Important questions and consideration like these are all part of the *cross-border life + wealth achievement conversation.* Answering them will define your cross-border lifestyle—whether you're "location independent" or your career or business is still tied to a geographic area—and allow you to be successful in your life and work. It is vital that your relationships, career or business and financial objectives are all in alignment with where you want to go in life and what you want to experience *from,* and provide *to,* our global village. The money you earn from using your skills, talents and experience, plus the financial capital you have built, should also align with and support your family and the causes that are important to you.

Working to sustain a lifestyle or starting or maintaining a family or a relationship is always demanding. Add one or more jurisdictions to that equation and the various, often labyrinthine, rules and regulations that come with living, investing and operating in these jurisdictions, plus navigating another way of life and language—and the daily stresses—are magnified exponentially. Leaving friends and family behind and embarking on a new career in a new country brings with it many questions and concerns. Will I be successful? Will my career flourish? Will my family life suffer? Will my children adjust? How will I navigate the new rules of the global economy? Five years from now will my career or my employer or my business be relevant?

These are many viable concerns that come with this life and lifestyle, but the future expansion of businesses and causes worldwide depends on people like you who have the drive and desire for adventure and for developing mutual beneficial relationships in our ever more connected world. The opportunities are there.

We're all dealing with some major struggles and challenges right now in life and we need something different—a new approach.

If you're like a lot of people I talk with you may be wondering: why should we limit ourselves to the life and financial strategies of our grandparents? It's time for us to move beyond the limitations of the industrial age. What we need is a new life and wealth model for modern global living.

I know because I went through the same struggles you may be facing. On a personal note, when I began my journey, I really had no idea of all the opportunities, all the challenges and the complexity – both personally and financially that I've described in this section. I believed in the traditional, industrial age model of life and wealth: go to school, get a job, save money for the future while trying to live a decent life today, and look forward to living "the good life" at some point in the future. I was used to "being different" from others having grown up on a farm in the midst of yacht and beach clubs, so I figured I was prepared for any potential social awkwardness, and I thought that my biggest challenge in life was going to be the life-altering decision-making process I completed at the age of 21: whether to decline the fantastic job offer I had received from a nationally recognized investment advisory firm and hope for the best with a long-distance relationship, or relocate (and thus get married to my fiancé).

I didn't know I could have so many options for personal and financial success and that all I needed was a different model. Frankly, I probably wouldn't have believed it if someone had told me.

But then I found myself in the middle of an identity and career crisis. After that I saw the global village through a different lens and discovered a new approach to thriving in it.

This book is my effort to lift the mist and guide you in.

INTRODUCTION

From Identity & Culture Clash to Building a New Model for Global Living

Tick…tick…tick. The minute hand on the clock on the credenza advances, breaking the silence. The sleek boardroom table separates me from Ed. Sue is standing at the window, staring at the orange sky as the sun sinks behind neighboring buildings.

I knew that if I didn't get home soon our nanny would be the one tucking my kids into bed — for the third time this week.

Although they were grateful for the career advancement and corporate perks, Ed and Sue were frustrated. They were looking for strategies to increase quality time with their family and to explore the hobbies their new lifestyle offered them. For the most part, they couldn't agree on their goals. One area where they did agree, was on their intent to remain overseas when the employment contract ended—they just didn't know where they wanted to end up or when that might take place. In the meantime, they wanted to talk about a strategy for the employer stock they were accumulating, conduct a thorough review of their estate plan particularly whether they needed a special needs trust of some kind for one of their children, and they wanted a strategy for assisting Sue's mother financially, starting in approximately three to five years. The strategies and wishes would need to navigate the rules of three countries excluding whatever country they wanted to end up in eventually.

I had earned three professional designations but they didn't prepare me to adequately answer the technical questions I was being asked that involved the international aspects of tax, marital and succession laws as well as how all the various laws work or don't work together between countries, all in addition to what professionals are supposed to do with that information once they have it. I had to research all of this on my own. I attended specialist conferences in international tax and estate planning. I obtained advanced training in investment consulting but none of these provided a step-by-step process. I even looked for a mentor but could not find one.

Back in the meeting room, I couldn't tell the clients, but what I was thinking to myself was 1) "I have the same problem. I don't have enough time with my kids and my husband either." 2) "I don't have any idea what to advise you to do about your personal matters. I just know how to advise you about your money", and 3) on the subject of money, "I have a ton of research to do, non-billable of course, before I can begin to advise you."

I was thirty-three with a five year old and a twelve month old. I had been living and working in my husband's birth country for ten years. During this period, my career had grown from selling investment products and providing financial plans to having a wealth management division under my direction. I had launched an association dedicated to advancing the financial planning profession also in my adopted country, but none of this prepared me for all the issues that I was confronting.

After reflecting on my client's concerns, I started wondering to myself "what if I focused the entire financial plan on what needed to happen, step by step, year by year in the client's life before I analyzed any of the typical technical financial planning areas? Would that approach allow me to create a flexible planning process? It seemed plausible, and in retrospect it seems obvious, yet none of my industry training told me just how to do that.

Just before I went home that night I was reminded that I had a training call the next day. I had heard about a new a life and business coach certification program while at a conference for financial planners. I decided to join the certification program believing this would be another perfunctory exercise on the path to another set of letters after my name, but what I got was a wake-up call that forever changed the way I looked at the world.

I found myself on the telephone.

After opening the class in the usual way, covering the objectives and how the class would be conducted, my confidence was higher than ever. Then our lead coach said five words that would change my life: "The client has the answers."

"Huh? Did I hear that right?"

I was consumed with this statement and other conflicting thoughts.

As I went through the program it became clear to me just how much I was not in control of my life. I started to realize how much I had been conditioned to think in a certain way. I had forgotten and almost lost a key part of myself because I had focused so much on trying to find my place among both the expat and local communities, neither of which were a true fit. And it became clear that my career — one that the textbooks told me was all about helping people achieve their dreams — was in reality, perpetuating the status quo of the Industrial Age. As I came to this realization I committed to that life and business-coaching program. It was no longer about the letters. It was about asking the hard questions. I realized I was living life by default, even though I thought I was designing. It turned out that I was designing within the confines of what others wanted or expected of me, not what I really wanted or what I wanted for my family. In the months that followed, I hired my first life and business coach, who helped me understand myself more. I realized that I needed to recalibrate my focus and this focus centered on four key questions:

First I wondered: "Am I living the way I *really* want to live?" It's true that I chose marriage and relocation but some part of me needed to go deeper: "Did I really choose it or had I thought of it as an opportunity that I didn't want to miss out on?"

Second: "Am I playing the way I want to play? Third: "Am I making a difference?" And fourth, "what about my work?" I was disillusioned. I used to question a lot of what was presented to me when I was growing up, yet here I was feeling as much shock as terror that I had somehow bought into the status quo. It was time to get back to questioning everything in my life. It was clear that I needed to create a new life and work model. And if I was going to stay in my industry, *I needed a new model for how I would serve in it.*

Once I was clear on what I thought I wanted I had to figure out "how could I consciously design and achieve the life that would allow me to live, work, play, and make a difference wherever in the world I want...when I want?" On a deeper level I wondered "could I arrange my work to live the way I want, use my skills to serve the world and still live life on my own terms? And if I could figure this out for myself, how would I communicate it to my husband? How would I approach it?"

As I moved through the questions and ran strategy through my head, I found myself re-designing my life—on paper. Nonetheless, my soul felt vindicated. I finally felt more connected to who I really was and how I wanted to connect to and affect the world. Part of that meant re-structuring my career. It also turned out that I needed to re-engineer the way I would serve in our global village, twice.

I share all this because I want you, dear reader, to know that I have been where you may be right now. Like you, I struggled with the notion of balancing life and making money, with fitting in socially and in my career. I also struggled through the process of building a plan with my husband—a plan that we both were excited about. A plan that would honor and fund both our joint and family goals, as well as our individual goals. In short, a plan that we could agree on.

But we did create that plan; a plan that saw me leave the broker-dealership where I had built my career. A plan that diverted $50,000 from our house renovation money to fund the start-up of an independent advisory firm dedicated to cross-border personal financial planning. A plan that originally put us on the path, and now sustains us living, working and playing where we want while making a difference for those we serve.

Those four questions were integral to how I restructured my financial planning approach and ultimately became the guide for how I transformed my approach to personal financial planning. I then implemented them in my strategies and resources for my clients and they too started achieving better results in their personal and financial life.

A Model Honed in the Trenches

In the ten years that followed, I started coaching a lot more, particularly helping clients understand the value of their human capital. After all, I get that it's hard to believe that who you are and what you know has value in the global marketplace. I know for sure that it does because once I started sharing my unique perspective and my specialized skills and knowledge everything shifted for me. People encouraged me to lecture so I started speaking at industry meetings. I wrote my first book, *When Families Cross Borders: A Guide for Internationally Mobile People* and it went on to price at over $2,000 a copy in the secondary market. You read that correctly — *over $2,000 dollars a copy*. The need for guidance in this area was so high that I couldn't keep up with the demand.

I discovered that the most sustainable plans were those *where the process itself focused less on the location specifics and more on the people and what needed to happen in their lives, first.* As I worked with more clients in various financial and lifestyle situations, I noticed they were struggling with solving the issues of portability. There was the assumption that our financial assets must move with us. I had to reconcile that against the fact that a lot of times they simply can't. Clients were coming to me for help in moving their financial assets and I was feeling compelled to ask them why. When they tried to answer my question it became clear that they really wanted help with tactics, yet I could see that wasn't where the *real* value was. We had to understand the *need* first.

Once we worked out the "why" we focused on the "how" by bringing the location specific opportunities and issues into the planning process. This makes sense when you understand that location specific opportunities and issues are *tactical*. Building our future based on tactics is backward because we don't account for changes in the economy and in our lives. When we don't account for lifestyle, family or economic changes the missteps are frustrating, expensive and hard to rebound from. Instead of spending our time focused on the activities that produce 20% of the result we want, we should spend our time focused on that *20% that produces 80%* of the result we *really* want.

What if we had a strategy where we could create comprehensive methodology based on what was most important in our life? A method that would allow us to mine the best opportunities around the world, that would consider our cultural imprints, and once all of this was factored in, would then consider the laws of all the relevant jurisdictions. Not only would it consider the laws, the methodology would analyze them in the context of whether we are relocating, settled but straddling more than one country, or repatriating and exiting the lifestyle.

What if this new approach to lifestyle, relationships and finances wouldn't limit us to the outdated lifestyle and financial strategies of our grandparents' day? Instead it would move us beyond the limitations of the Industrial Age and even beyond borders. What we would achieve is a new way of life, and a wealth model for modern global living.

Think about that for a moment. What would your life be like if you had a plan that catered to your needs and the needs of your family; one that created the life you dreamt of, that you and your partner could agreed on? A plan that you both understood and could implement? A plan that was dynamic, not something that you created once. A plan that was flexible, not something that you created all over again from scratch, year after year, location by location. A plan that considered implementation of its strategies and tactics across countries and currencies from the beginning rather than trying to fit them in later. That's what you'll find in the pages that follow.

I want to be respectful of your time, so I've structured the book to deliver enough of what you need without covering *all* the possible technical issues you may face. It's true that you need to save and invest money and it's true that tax and estate planning is complicated, but none of that matters if you don't have a plan for your life. It's self-defeating to think that a cross-border financial plan-- the very type of plans I have been creating with clients for nearly twenty years— has to start with the technical planning areas. In fact, in my experience, this is the wrong order, unless you are seeking specific financial information. Let's get started.

SECTION ONE

YOUR LIFE + WEALTH

In this section I want to paint a picture of the landscape that you and I are traversing together. This is about the next part of a journey you have already started. The Industrial Age is history. The opportunities and realities of the Information Age are here. It's no longer a situation of waiting for the world to shift, it's now about clearing the mist so that you can see where you are right now so that you can see where and how you fit. Once you know where you are, you'll be in a great place to determine your next step.

In the next chapter I will begin lifting the mist on our life and lifestyle, and then, in the following chapter, I'll address the difference between the terms global and cross-border for our purposes, and I'll explain cross-border personal financial planning in detail. In the final chapter of this section, I'll introduce the model and methodology that we explore more closely in Section Two.

1

LIFE IN THE GLOBAL VILLAGE

Our personal, work and financial lives have transitioned from a traditional one into a global one, yet we don't have the tools to fully grasp all the options available to us or understand how to avoid the myriad pitfalls that can endanger our finances and even our relationships as we cross borders.

But why is this the case? And why is personal financial planning typically the most neglected aspect of this life and lifestyle? To understand the answers to these questions, we need to understand what I call the "Four Dynamics of Global Living"[1]

The Four Dynamics of Global Living

1. Global Opportunities Are Within Our Personal Reach

In the old Industrial Age and in lifestyles that are localized the direct impact of globalization on us as individuals is marginal. In the Information Age, globalization continues to push economic progress *internationally*. New vocabulary such as "global nomad" or "third culture kids" has been introduced to help us understand some of the unique aspects and by-products of this new reality. And old, outdated terms like "expat" are giving way to new terms like "triangle" and "cross-border" to better reflect modern day.

In his book *The World is Flat*, Thomas L. Friedman described the "three great eras of globalization" and the "dynamic force" behind each era. Although all three eras are important in understanding the global dynamics that underlie the global village and the financial

---

[1] The Four Dynamic of Global Living were originally published by Jennifer Patterson as "Four Dynamics of Cross-Border Living" in *When Families Cross Borders: A Guide for Internationally Mobile People*, 2006.

planning issues addressed by this book, it is what Friedman calls "Globalization 3.0" that contributes to the need for us to understand how our personal and business planning must change as a result of crossing a country border—either physically, via investment or via partnership or business. In "Globalization 3.0", individuals must, and can now ask, "where do I fit into the global competition and opportunities of the day and how can I, on my own, collaborate with others globally?"[2]

Today, we can consciously design a life that allows us to live, work, play and make a difference from anywhere in the world.

This means:

- Your knowledge, your skills and your experience have greater market value than you probably ever imagined.

- You can live, work, play and make a difference anywhere in the world, and the best way to do that is to use your knowledge and experience to help others succeed.

- You can get paid for using your skills and knowledge, either physically or virtually, and in the process you can build economic and location independence as well as claim more time for your family, your hobbies, personal growth or whatever else you desire.

Living this way is like moving into a neighborhood or a village. Welcome to your new village. We call it the global village.[3]

In the global village, the traditional life and work model our grandparents followed is no longer relevant. We no longer need to

---

[2] Friedman, Thomas L., *The World is Flat: A Brief History of the Twenty-First Century* (New York: Farrar, Straus and Giroux) p. 9

[3] The term was coined by Marshall McLuhan in his books *The Gutenberg Galaxy: The Making of Typographic Man* (1962) and *Understanding Media* (1964)

follow the so-called "deferred life plan" where we wait until we reach some magical stop work date to begin *living*.

This is because although the world may be becoming increasingly "flat," the people who run it are multicultural and multidimensional.

2. We are Multidimensional

Most cultures and philosophies will agree on four universal dimensions of life that meet our basic needs and motivations: *to live, to love, to learn and to leave a legacy*. Now more than ever, internationally mobile people and their families are seeking ways to find balance among these dimensions.

The increasing pace of work and life has increased stress on the family unit. More women are taking their careers across international borders and men are taking on more responsibilities at home, causing relationship dynamics to shift. Roles in the family have become fluid. With advances in technology, the men and women who have more of the direct responsibilities with the family are starting location-independent businesses. They are working remotely or working from home.

What we need in our lives to experience lasting fulfillment has dramatically changed. Men and women are now seeking greater authenticity and personal expression. The days of women being required to be financially dependent on men, as well as men carrying the burden of providing for his family alone, are gone. This change has created incredible new opportunities, both for us as individuals and as a couple. As individuals, we have the opportunity to be ourselves in ways we couldn't before, allowing for relationships to be more intimate and profound and allowing us to have the impact we most want to make, whether that is personally, in our family life, socially, in our local communities or in our global village.

As we all know, where you have family and relationships you have the potential for conflict. When you add in the elements of the global village, it compounds the frequency and the magnitude of the potential for conflict.

3. Cultural and Familial Imprints Regarding Life, Money, and Wealth

Each of us has many maps in our head. They can be divided into two main categories: maps of the way things are and maps of the way things should be. We interpret everything through these mental maps. We seldom question their accuracy; we're often unaware that we even have them. We simply assume that the way we see things is the way they *really* are or the way they *should* be. *The way we see things is the source of the way we think and the way we act.*

Our upbringing and the culture in which we were raised provide a filter through which we see life.

Cultural anthropologist and author of *The Culture Code,* Clotaire Rapaille explains "the Culture Code is the unconscious meaning we apply to any given thing...via the culture in which we are raised." He continues, "It is obvious to everyone that cultures are different from one another. What most people don't realize; however, is that these differences actually lead to our processing the same information in different ways."[4]

Rapaille's research and discovery of cultural codes ties to Henri Laborit, "who drew a clear connection between learning and emotion, showing that without the latter the former was impossible. The stronger the emotion, the more clearly an experience is learned. The combination of the experience and its accompanying emotion creates something known widely as an imprint, a term first applied

---

[4] Rapaille, Clotaire, *The Culture Code* (New York: Broadway Books) pp. 5-6

by Konrad Lorenz. Once an imprint occurs it strongly conditions our thought processes and shapes our future actions. Each imprint helps make us more of who we are. The combination of imprints defines us."[5]

Imprints relating to financial matters are known as *money messages*. These messages stem from stated and un-stated attitudes, lessons and reactions that we have collected along our life journey. These messages are often shaped by the words our family members used as well as their behaviors. As with the cultural imprint, the degree of acuity of money imprint is tied to the level of emotion felt when the imprint took place. Those belief systems, buried deeply within our subconscious, can be traced back to childhood. Some messages are positive while others are not.

Recognition of our belief systems has powerful consequences — positive and negative — on all aspects of our lives. Conflicts about role, money and wealth are really conflicting scripts. I call these *life + wealth scripts* and we'll take a closer look at this in Chapter 10, Cross-Border Life + Wealth Mindset.

The opportunities of the global village also bring significant new challenges. We must learn to successfully communicate our new needs and how to support our partners' new needs as they do the same for us. We must learn to create financial equity in the relationship and distinguish it from ownership percentages and the notion of equality. We must also learn to recognize our cultural and familial imprints regarding money, wealth, work and roles, and to support our partners' in their recognition.

If you read articles discussing cross-border personal financial planning, you will probably recognize the next Dynamic because this is where most attention is focused.

---

[5] Ibid. p. 6

4. Laws are Jurisdictional

Despite some international conventions, laws are jurisdictional. More specifically, although the world is increasingly "flat," tax, matrimonial and succession laws are still defined by national boundaries. This means that if you own assets or have family members living in more than one country you can't assume that the laws that apply to those assets, or to the people resident in another country, apply the same way. We must understand that these different areas of law are defined by national and local boundaries and sometimes by citizenship so we can make good decisions.

While the words may be similar across country borders the laws that apply to the words may be *very* different. Because a financial product is called a "qualified retirement plan" in two countries does not mean that the tax law associated with each of those countries match one another. Because you settle a trust in one jurisdiction does not mean that the laws that apply to that trust in that jurisdiction will be upheld, or that the trust will even be recognized, in another. The regulations that apply to financial products and financial advice are different in each jurisdiction. We can't assume that a professional competent in the rules of one jurisdiction knows how those rules change when a person leaves that jurisdiction. Similarly, we can't assume that a professional can comprehensively advise someone of a different nationality entering the jurisdiction in which they are licensed to practice.

This is where conflict is the *norm*, rather than the *exception*. It is deceiving to the traveler who has not been briefed.

The 4 Dynamics help us maintain perspective when it comes to creating a personal financial plan for our life in the Global Village. We'll take a closer look at this statement in the next chapter, but for our purposes right now, consider that all but one of the Dynamics are effectively global, and consider that all of the Dynamics, except the fact that despite some global conventions, the laws that affect the financial and legal aspects of our personal financial plans tie to what we want our plan to achieve.

For example, if we physically relocate to another jurisdiction do our cultural and familial imprints change? Not likely. Similarly the fact that we are multidimensional beings with different levels of need really ties to our goals and aspirations in life. Because this comes from within us those needs follow us no matter where we are physically. And the issue of global opportunities also ties to our goals and aspirations. Thus three of The 4 Dynamics are strategic issues and therefore are not changing very significantly when we physically relocate across a country border. Taking advantage of opportunities, our needs at different points in time, and our imprinting tie primarily to mindset. Thus global living is not a destination in and of itself. It's a journey, driven by a philosophy and way of living.

Quite often, internationally mobile people, their families, and their businesses feel caught between their dreams and goals, and the complexities that come with navigating the rules of more than one country.

This is partially due to the way that financial services are delivered and partially due to the lack of an adequate planning methodology when our lives become "cross-border".

At this point you're probably trying to draw a distinction between "global" and "cross-border", so let's shift our attention there now...

Global versus Cross-Border

A common area of confusion relates to distinctions between the term "global" and the term "cross-border." The dictionary tells us they both are adjectives so they must be interchangeable, right? Not really.

According to the *Oxford Dictionary of English*:

- **Global** is an adjective, "relating to the whole world; worldwide 'the global economy.'"[6]

- **Cross-border** is also an adjective, defined as "involving movement or activity across a border between two countries".[7]

So, the term *global* refers to the entire world, whereas *cross-border* really refers more specifically to activity or movement across a border, physical or not, between two countries. Thus, we can serve people globally but the rules that tell us how to tax the income earned from serving those people are going to be determined according to the rules of where we and/or our company are located, where the delivery of the service or sale takes place and where the buyer is located at the time of delivery of the service, or where the buyer resides, and how that country looks at the transaction. In other words, the conduct of business with that person wherever they are in the world (your global customer or client) is cross-border because there is a transaction taking place between different countries, involving people in different countries.

As you will see in another example when I address taxation, you can have an investment portfolio that invests "globally", meaning it is free to invest anywhere in the world it chooses, but the tax on the income earned from what the portfolio invests in will be dependent on the rules (often a tax treaty to prevent double taxation) that exist between the country where the investment originates and the country in which you are resident.

---

[6] Anon, (2018). In: 1st ed. [online] Available at:
https://en.oxforddictionaries.com/definition/global [Accessed 16 Jan. 2018].
[7] Anon, (2018). In: 1st ed. [online] Available at:
https://en.oxforddictionaries.com/definition/cross-border [Accessed 16 Jan. 2018].

You: Single Country or Cross-Border?

As the simplified example above illustrates, it's important for you to recognize both when, and how, you become "cross-border."

If you live in one country, are a citizen of one country, are single, have assets located in the country in which you live, and none of your personal goals involve another country or a cause in another country, then you are probably "single country" and thus a "single-country personal financial plan" is probably sufficient.

But when your life and the facts associated with your life, your lifestyle and your financial assets expand beyond one country's border you most likely become "cross-border." Let's take a closer look at this:

The 2 Meta Scenarios and the Cross-Border Living Transitions

In my experience there are two interrelated concepts that you need to understand when it comes to locating where you are in this world and thus how your personal financial planning is affected.

First, there is what I call "The 2 Meta Scenarios".

The 2 Meta Scenarios

Straddle is when you are settled in a planning scenario but you may be *straddling* locations literally due to part-time residence in more than one place or country, or due to citizenship and assets in more than one country. As the word straddle implies, your facts and circumstances have you involved in more than one country but you are not in the physical process of a relocating. You're not re-settling somewhere else for now. You are cross-border.

Single Country is when you are settled in a planning scenario but your life, your career or business and your financial assets are confined to one country. Sometimes you hear this planning referred to as a "domestic financial plan" or a "single-country personal financial plan."

You either transition from "single country" into "straddle" or you are born into "straddle", meaning when you are born you are a dual- or even a tri-national citizen (that is a citizen of two or three countries simultaneously).

Second, there are transition types or periods that must keep in mind. I call them *Cross-Border Living Transitions*. The technical issues and action items are typically grouped by fact set. Specifically: relocation, straddle and exit.

The Cross-Border Living Transitions

Relocation will require some kind of inbound and outbound planning for the new location of residence, and possibly domicile (I cover how residence and domicile are different in chapter 6).

Exit is when your facts and circumstances change from *straddle* to "single country". It may be a birth country or a country where you have decided to consolidate your life. Some families exit the cross-border lifestyle while others do not. This situation and financial plan type can also come into consideration when a dual national formally renounces citizenship of one country (aka "expatriates").

Let's look at two hypothetical examples to illustrate how these concepts come together:

Single Country A to Single Country B

You are born in Country A. You live, work and have financial assets in Country A. You have a single country plan for Country A. You decide that you want to accept a job offer in Country B. Your country of citizenship does not tax you on worldwide income and/or assets once you no longer meet their definition of resident and domicile. You liquidate all of your financial assets in Country A and you move that cash with you to Country B where you confine your life and your financial assets to that country.

This simple fact pattern supports a transition plan from Country A to Country B. Questions and issues arise to ensure that you completely exit Country A and obtain nonresident status. You then create a personal financial plan based on the rules and regulations of Country B.

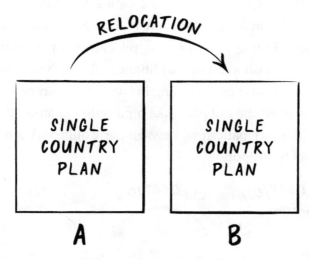

What if we vary one fact in this scenario such that you become a resident of Country B because of work and other facts but you also remain a resident, albeit perhaps a part-time resident, of Country A, what if anything changes? You can see that this change in pattern supports a relocation/transition plan from Single Country A to Straddle AB. Meaning you are now going to need a cross-border plan that considers the rules of both Country A and Country B.

Single Country A to Straddle AB to Straddle ABC to Single Country A

Let's now show how the planning might evolve over multiple years and three jurisdictions. Taking the previous scenario, let's pick up from the variation. So to recap, that means we had a single country plan for Country A, we then created a relocation plan into a cross-border plan covering countries A and B. Now, we have accepted a job offer in Country C. We have assets that we cannot, or choose not, to liquidate in both countries A an B and we now have some family responsibilities in Country A as well that we cover financially. We now need to review our cross-border financial plan (Straddle AB) to consider what needs to change, etc. to cover residency etc. in Country C. Thus creating Straddle ABC. Finally, after some additional time we decide that we have had enough of the cross-border lifestyle and want to relocate permanently back to Country A and wish to set up our financial life such that we have no assets or responsibilities remaining in any other country. In this final situation we build the exit plan (aka repatriation plan) so that we can end up in the fact pattern of new Single Country A and a single country plan to support it.

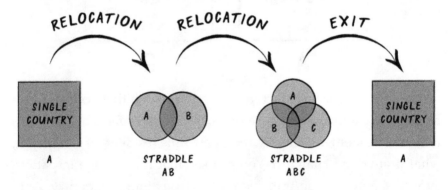

When life introduces more than one set of rules, as is the case in cross-border living, navigation becomes more difficult. With all the opportunities, all the rules and conflicts of some rules between countries, and the rules that come from culture and how we were raised, along with finding agreement on what you want for yourself, what your partner wants for him or herself, and what you want for your family, it can be overwhelming. So, it helps to see the collection of facts, goals and dreams on a timeline when we are in design mode.

The chart below shows a hypothetical timeline where a family is presently abroad and anticipates a relocation to another country in years four and eleven. There is also an expectation to return to full-time living in a single country. Two key goals are also represented, specifically funding university costs and funding or providing support for a loved one. You can see how they coincide with the transition periods.

PLAN TIMELINE WITH META SCENARIOS AND TRANSITION PERIODS

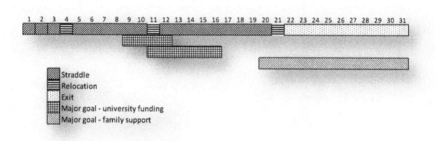

So while you may be globally minded your personal financial plan is cross-border when your nationality, your assets, your physical location and often your family involve more than one country.

The point of these examples and this section of the book is to help you recognize when a major plan restructure— sometimes with more emphasis at the tactical, jurisdictionally-specific, sometimes at both the strategic and tactical levels—may be required.

It is also to help you recognize that each of these periods. And the transitions themselves, require personal financial planning processes that are slightly different in their approach. The specific ways the approaches differ are beyond the scope of this book; however, it is important to distinguish between the approaches and how they come into being because, as I will discuss, as the financial planning profession matures globally and more and more advisors enter the specialty field of cross-border personal financial planning, being able to distinguish how the various advisors operate their business and how they build personal financial plans is important. By being able to locate yourself and understand this world, you will be better equipped to find and use the professional assistance.

2

PERSONAL FINANCIAL PLANNING
IN THE GLOBAL VILLAGE

The Financial Planning Profession is Still Evolving

As the personal financial planning profession has emerged globally through the establishment of non-profit organizations who seek to educate people about the value of unbiased advice without the pressure of the purchase of a product, and to develop and operate professional certification and education programs to ensure worldwide professional standards in financial planning, a plethora of titles and certifications have been introduced. This, in addition to the fact that just about anyone can use the title "financial planner," is causing confusion about who is qualified to give advice and on what aspect of comprehensive financial planning they are qualified.

Today, the CERTIFIED FINANCIAL PLANNER, ("CFP®"), certification program is the oldest and represents "global excellence in financial planning" across 26 territories globally.[8]

But, cross-border personal financial planning is still a highly specialized area and thus is still not part of the curriculum of CFP certification programs. So while the letters are a mark of distinction in personal financial planning, it doesn't mean that a professional bearing the mark has any education and or experience in cross-border personal financial planning. The saying "buyer beware" applies.

---

[8] At the end of 2016, there were over 170,000 CFP professionals worldwide. For more information including links to the nonprofit member organizations around the world, visit www.fpsb.org

About Cross-Border Personal Financial Planning

It's my experience that most people focus on their financial matters episodically and in segments. This is due, in large part, to the way that financial services in general are delivered: non-collaboratively and separately. For example, the estate planner hopes to effectively transfer wealth to the next generation while the investment advisor hopes to maximize returns in relation to risk, and the tax advisor seeks to minimize transfer and annual income taxes.

Each of these individual advisors may give you sound advice when viewed in the limited context of that discipline. While this may have worked in the past, particularly in situations limited to one country, actions taken in one area have an impact on another area. Absent the reconciliation and integration of all of these segments, the result is a disconnected set of ideas that typically conflict with one another. Since the rules of various countries also typically conflict with one another, the potential for conflict across strategies, the probability of high advisory fees and the inability to make decisions is exacerbated in the cross-border context.

What is Cross-Border Personal Financial Planning?

Cross-border personal financial planning is "the process through which coordinated, comprehensive strategies and techniques are developed and implemented as a result of analysis of the laws of two or more countries to achieve the client's goals and objectives"[9]

Cross-border personal financial planning is thus the process of making strategic decisions for your wealth based on what is important in your life, across all the country borders that are relevant.

---

[9] First introduced by Jennifer Patterson in a presentation at the national conference of the Financial Planning Association 2007; adapted from the definition of personal financial planning created by the College For Financial Planning, now the National Endowment for Financial Education (NEFE).

The Exponential Nature of Cross-Border Complexity

Imagine that there are five key areas of personal finance where decisions may need to be made (e.g., cash management, tax and tax return preparation, gifting and charity, estate and legal, and investing). Now, imagine that your personal life (including your career or your business), spans three countries. Take the three countries and multiply that by the five key areas of personal finance and you have at least 15 areas where decision fatigue and overwhelm are easily found. I refer to this as the "Exponential Nature of Cross-Border Complexity". To harness it, we just need to learn the formula.

Does Your Cross-Border Financial Plan Serve Your Life?

Sometimes we are caught between dreams and borders, at least that is how it can feel.

If you haven't yet reached a cross-border life of your design it's not necessarily because you're doing the wrong things. Living such a life means you're coming from your strongest self. Your mind, your body, your relationships and your daily activities all seem to hit the mark. Some people never experience that.

But right now, you kind of have to, right? I mean, think about the major challenges we're facing in our lives. We're all dealing with fatigue. We're overwhelmed. There's a lot of stress. We're trying lots of things, but perhaps we're not getting the progress, the breakthroughs and the fulfillment that we really want. It's possible that fatigue is happening because of distractions but also because there are a lot of opportunities available to us right now.

There's also a lot of fear. We may be fearful and stressed because we may not be ready, or think we're ready, for what's next. We're worried that we won't be able to deal with life's challenges because life seems to be getting more chaotic. This stress makes us feel overwhelmed. Or maybe you're fearful that after all these years you're still not where you thought you'd be. Perhaps you thought you'd be so much further along. Or the real fear is that you're stuck, and you're wondering, *is this is all there is*? We often attribute this fear to depression. But it's really fear that the life you're living isn't what you wanted, dreamed or imagined your life would be like.

What stops us from achieving that life? What do we fear most? One of our greatest fears is uncertainty. One of the questions I pose a lot, particularly when working with a client who has a lot of options and a lot of complexity with those options is, "what can we flip from an unknown to a known?" We simply cannot plan when we have too many variables.

One of the more common challenges we face with cross-border financial planning is the issue of certainty when it comes to planning for the future. In my experience, there are two ways this challenge is typically approached. The first is using a strategy of replicating today's lifestyle exactly in a single number (or a percentage of it), applying a rate of inflation and projecting this out into the future. *This approach makes the numbers the primary focus (we'll call that "W" for money or wealth) with less focus on what the numbers represent (we'll call that "L" for life).* If we imagine a future based on this strategy, it typically looks like this:

$$W_L$$

A similar approach is to rely on short-term action only (typically, because of a future we can't see, fear, or often a lack of agreement or commitment). In this case, we might focus one year on building wealth, the next three on lifestyle, and the fifth year on building wealth with a complete start over with regard to financial tactics, and so on...

$$W_L \quad w_L \quad w_L \quad w_L \quad W_L \ldots$$

Suddenly, ten or more years have gone by and when we stop to measure where we are, it typically looks like this:

W L,

versus where we want to be, which is:

W L

Both of these approaches have severe limitations, typically resulting in even bigger problems arising when we have fewer options for mitigating them.

But what if we look at things differently? What if, as we consider opportunities, we also consider the tactical issues that arise together with any resulting changes required? What if we then mix in what we most want to see take place in the key areas of our lives, along with how we manage the pressures of society, family, and others? What if we stopped seeing The 4 Dynamics as separate and independent of one another and start seeing them as symbiotic?

THE 4 DYNAMICS - REIMAGINED

Very often we approach financial planning matters from a practical standpoint. This may seem to be perfectly logical. After all, you may read a checklist that suggests a number of practical items to be considered and resolved. For instance, you need to review your will in the context of the countries involved (or create one), and protect your family from the loss of income should you or your spouse die. These emotional and practical needs require attention. So you consult a professional. Perhaps you determine that you need life insurance. The life insurance agent decides to focus on the "what." For example, what is the goal that you want to achieve? What is the amount of insurance that you need? You answer the questions in the order presented: "I want to protect my family and I don't know. Can you help me figure that out?" You then listen to the benefits of the various products the agent can provide you. You consider the different types of policies and how the policies may benefit you in achieving your goal. Finally, you walk away with a life insurance policy, feeling good about your decision — an increased feeling of peace of mind passes through you and you feel relieved — it's over and done with!

Time passes. You've been dutifully paying your premiums, but a number of things have changed since you first bought the policy and you begin to question the coverage at every premium payment.

Eventually, you may end up in my office and I ask why you bought the policy. Remembering the conversation with the agent, you tell me that you bought it to protect your family. You were concerned that if something happened to you the savings that you and your spouse had accumulated would not support your family. After all, your spouse may have left a career to allow you to take this international posting. Maybe you also had a large mortgage on your house and you didn't know how your family would pay the mortgage and property taxes, buy groceries, and maintain the home.

You don't know how long it would take your spouse to find a job and if the income it would be enough to support the family. And you don't know how the assets would be assessed for estate tax purposes. Ultimately you knew that you had to do something. It's clear that you value your family and you want to take care of them. It's also clear how those values—protecting your family—drove the objective and ultimately the action taken—getting life insurance.

Logic suggests that it doesn't make sense to move to the technical design phase of the financial planning process before clear objectives are determined about the reason you need it. Similarly, it is difficult to execute the necessary documentation that brings a plan into action, until you actually have a *clearly defined series of objectives and strategies to support those objectives.* Nonetheless, in my practice, in both a cross-border context and a domestic context, I've witnessed these illogical initiatives attempted on a regular basis. Plans are designed without clear objectives and various strategies are implemented before an overall, strategic plan is in place.

Unfortunately, as a result of not putting the necessary effort into this step, many people, with assets in various countries, have been caught in a paradox of choice, resulting in the constant evaluation of different tactics. They consider one idea after another, after consulting with an expert who raises another issue to consider. The client grows frustrated and may abandon the planning altogether. While he or she has been asked to consider what a particular tactic will do, neither the advisors nor the client has considered why they are seeking the strategies.

Frozen by Fear

A highly successful professional, and a dual-national client, I'll call her Ann, was plagued by all of her "what if?" questions. When we first met for a preliminary meeting she wanted to get down to all of the various possible scenarios: What if we decide to retire to another country altogether? Should I renounce my U.S. citizenship? After all, I'm still a national of this country. After ten years of living here, I still have some assets in my birth country. Ultimately, Ann was unable to take any kind of action in relation to her family's financial planning because of her fear of making a mistake. This fear was compounded because Ann was attempting to provide solutions to *all* of her *real* and *potential issues* at the same time. She was frozen by fear.

Education funding for Ann's children was an important goal. So, when I posed the question of where the children (who are also dual nationals but have never lived in the United States) would want to pursue their university education (this is important to determine how to structure the investments for this goal), it met with a very patriotic — "the U.S., of course!" After considering the fact that at least one of her children might prefer a European university experience, Ann fell back to a general feeling of frustration and despair.

We began the planning stage with Ann and her husband by focusing on their core values and asking them to hold a family meeting to allow everyone to express some of their individual goals. We were able to narrow options as a result of this discussion. We then shifted attention to understanding their immediate concerns and their current immigration and financial situation. Once they had this context, Ann was able to ease into a collaborative process of designing a financial plan.

It's vital to understand that we can plan for uncertainty. That is ultimately the point of planning. Successful planning; however, requires that we to build in flexibility. We build in flexibility using two steps, which I will introduce after I address a very common problem with planning in general, particularly in the cross-border context.

Most people are building personal financial plans and then trying to have a life. But this is backward. While professionals may be the "expert" in the area in which they are technically proficient, you are the expert on your life. Effective and meaningful financial planning, particularly in a cross-border context, requires the collaboration of both experts.

But if you are reading this book, you're already intrigued by the idea that there is a next level for you. In your well being, in your relationships and of course there is a next level financially. There's a next level for you to achieve and you know it. This isn't so much that you're doing all the wrong things but sometimes there are better things for you to focus on. There are better strategies for you to put into play. Knowing what those are is a differentiator and that's what I've spent my life as an expat partner and in my career as a cross-border financial planner figuring out.

What would your life be like if you had a series of strategies that were based on what is truly important to you, where your financial assets were working in harmony with your social and personal aims, short-term and long-term? Take a moment to imagine that.

Before you build your business plan or your personal financial plan, build your life plan. Where are you living and why? Is this where you want to live? How are you enjoying life? Do you have any kind of major key life events you need to think through? How and where is education slotting into your life, either for you or your children? Once you know this you can build your personal financial plan around them using the steps outlined in this book. When that's complete, build out the business plan (or career plan) around all of your criteria. How do you go about this? I'm glad you asked.

3
OVERVIEW OF THE MODEL AND METHODOLOGY FOR MODERN CROSS-BORDER PERSONAL FINANCIAL PLANNING

It all starts with a strategic plan for your life that, as part of the development process, initially takes the view that you can live anywhere and thus, considers your life as though you're not tied to the laws of any jurisdiction.

Life + Wealth Achievement Formula™

The *Life + Wealth Achievement Formula* is the counterintuitive approach to financial success without wrecking your life. Although it's a method (meaning that it's a repeatable process with predictable outcomes), the application of the process is dynamic. What this means is we are able to *refine, optimize* and *adapt* with each new application *as well as what we discover through its implementation*. It's not a rigid, predestined, one-option-only plan but rather a structure from which to create the future of your choice. It's flexible, while keeping the perspective of where you are in the three phases of the wealth life cycle: *accumulation, preservation* and *transfer*. It allows you to circle back to another path or start blazing a new one altogether.

Philosophy

An underlying philosophy of *Life + Wealth Achievement Formula* is that wealth is the sum of our human, social and financial capital as individuals. When two individuals elect to join their life journeys, they become a family. Thus family wealth is the sum of the combined human, social and financial capital.

Think of wealth as a Venn diagram— three closed circles that overlap—with you at the center. As you will see when I explain how we shift over our lifetimes from a place of zero or lower wealth to a level of having sufficient wealth to support ourselves and our families from financial capital alone, and finally into a level of being able to leave a financial legacy, your financial capital is a tool to support the growth of your human and social capital and financial capital is created from the use of your human and social capital.

THE 3 DIMENSIONS OF WEALTH

SOCIAL CAPITAL

HUMAN CAPITAL

FINANCIAL CAPITAL

YOU

Social capital can be summarized as connections to others. Where our social capital overlaps with our human capital, it produces social connections that can support our life. Where our social capital overlaps with our financial capital, is where we make a difference in the lives of others.

A central tenet of *Life + Wealth Achievement Formula* is that wealth supports your life it doesn't *drive it*. At the same time; however, wealth is a *tool* to support the growth of our human and social capital.

Traditionally, life and wealth were seen as equal sides—requiring tradeoffs to stay in balance. The truth is each is a part of the puzzle and they do not need to be equal all the time with regard to how we allocate money, time and attention.

The secret is to shift from "either/or thinking" to "both/and thinking." Think of the philosophy as "cross-training" for your life and wealth.

YOUR LIFE + WEALTH SUPPORT ONE ANOTHER USING THE 5 A'S OF ACHIEVEMENT

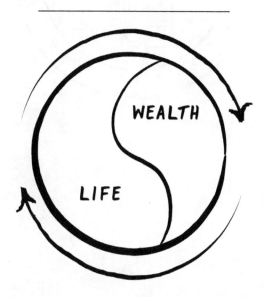

The goal of cross training in sport and in business is improving overall performance. Our goal is the same here. We're looking for sustainable success.

And thus we come to the system in its full glory:

The illustration below shows the pillars of *Life + Wealth Achievement Formula* with *The 5 A's of Achievement*.

LIFE + WEALTH ACHIEVEMENT FORMULA™ WITH THE 5 A'S OF ACHIEVEMENT

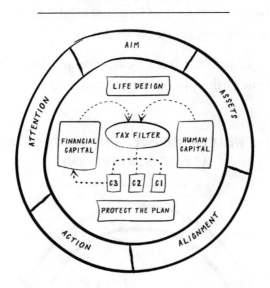

The pillars of the system are:

1. Life Design

2. Human Capital

3. Financial Capital

4. Tax Filter

5. Cash Design

6. Plan Protection

Three of these areas: human capital, tax filter, and cash design, are the key areas for the creation of wealth for ourselves and for our families. Financial capital is the key area for the sustaining of the wealth we create. All of us have more control over these areas than we think.

Let's demystify how financial capital is made.

Using the Model to Achieve Financial Freedom

How is financial capital created? Is it all about investing wisely? Getting the right asset class mix? Choosing the right asset types? Finding the next best idea to produce the top return for the period? In the world I come from, some people would have you focus on only those things. I'm not suggesting that they don't have a role to play, but for now, let's just ignore all that investment noise and start from the beginning. Please indulge me for a couple of minutes while we head to math class. I think this is the easiest way to convey my point.

Put simply:

Financial capital, FC, created from human capital is given by the simplified equation.

$$FC = HC + E,$$

where we use our energy (E) to convert our human capital (HC) into financial capital.

But how does this happen? We can drill down on this formula to see that there are three steps, starting with the creation of money (M):

First, the combination of our human capital (HC) and our energy (E) create money, (M), as shown in the equation below where M is substituted in for FC.

$$M = HC + E,$$

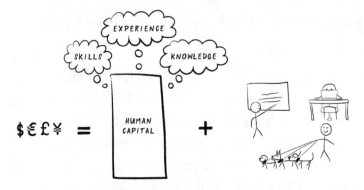

Second, the money (M) we earn is reduced by taxes (T) to arrive at Net Earned Income (NEI).

$$NIE = (M - T)$$

Net Earned Income (NEI) is also known as the money (M) you have available for spending on fixed expenses (C1), discretionary expenses (C2), as well as money you can set aside for the future, in the form of short-to mid-term expenses (SME) and savings (S), that you will convert to FC, (C3).

We often refer to the allocation of net income as cash flow. I will explain the 3 C's of Cash Flow in a later chapter, but I include them here now for context.

Third, Net Earned Income is allocated to the 3 C's of Cash Flow in a way that best supports our life and wealth, remembering that C3 is made up of a further allocation of Net Earned Income (NEI) between savings (S) and money set aside for short- and mid-term expenses (SME) as shown by the following equations.

$$NEI = (C1 + C2) + C3, \text{ and}$$

$$C3 = S + SME$$

Finally, financial capital, FC, is produced when savings is mixed with *Life + Wealth* investing as shown by the equation.

S + *Life + Wealth Achievement Investing* → FC

Life + Wealth Achievement Formula looks like this when we show all the pillars working together.

LIFE + WEALTH ACHIEVEMENT FORMULA™ SHOWING THE FLOW OF MONEY BETWEEN FOUR SYSTEM PILLARS

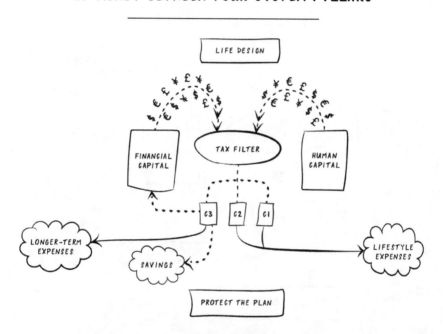

Now that we know how to create financial capital, let's talk about why creating it is so important: financial independence.

How do you know when you've reached financial independence? You have reached the point of financial independence when you have sufficient financial capital that can, at a minimum, replace the income you can earn from deploying your human capital.

When we are financially independent, the plan may reflect a reduction, if not elimination, of the production of income from human capital. At that time, we may be directing human capital to community and causes. This is illustrated below:

LIFE + WEALTH ACHIEVEMENT FORMULA™ SHOWING THE USE OF INCOME SOLELY FROM FINANCIAL CAPITAL

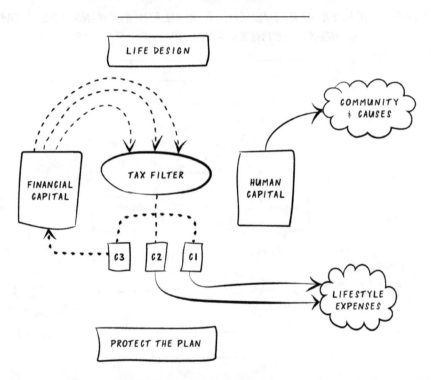

The goal is to build financial capital that provides what we call passive income. Passive income can come in various forms: rent, royalties, licensing fees and business income from intellectual property, dividends, interest.

If we want to build a financial legacy, then our goal is to build financial capital that produces passive income at the level of some multiple of lifestyle expenses. The multiple is goal dependent but could range from as little as two times lifestyle expenses to ten times or more.

A Better Approach

Because the cross-border lifestyle is deliberately open to how we want to design our lives, we need a dynamic, ongoing planning process that can be chunked down into short-term action plan(s).

One of the important aspects of the methodology is while there is a repeatable process with predictable outcomes; the application of the method is dynamic, not static. This is a reality that is often overlooked by many. The truth is, change is constant so the methodology not only anticipates this reality, it embraces and expects it. Thus, with each application of the method, we are able to refine, and optimize based on what new information we provide and what we discover from the previous implementation.

In personal financial planning, all too often, many of the processes are carried out—and the same assumptions with them—year in and year out, because they were done in the prior year. Then, we lament about how our plan is detrimentally affected by "unforeseen circumstances" and we often give up on planning altogether. Yet, if we looked closer, we'd see that we didn't take enough time at the design phase of the planning to realize that *the numbers are a function of design.* If we just apply last year's numbers to this year, how can we really expect anything different from last year? In a single-country planning scenario, you may be able to overcome this challenge but in the cross-border plan, this problem can be much harder to recover from.

The other common problem is that short-term planning considered only the end of the current year as if next year did not exist, or if it does exist, it exists as a replication of the current year. All totaled, the short-term plan really only exists to determine how much we need to save now for the future, typically the artificial finish line called "retirement."

We take control using the "5 A's".

The 5 A's of Achievement

The 5 A's typically work together as shown in formula format below as a standalone annual process:

$$((AIM + ASSETS) * ALIGNMENT) + ACTION + ATTENTION$$

The 5 A's of Achievement can also be used in connection with each of the pillars of Life + Wealth Achievement Formula™. Let's take a closer look at each of the 5 A's.

ASSETS. This includes your human capital—your skills, your knowledge, your experience, which is all about your ability to generate income through your career or through entrepreneurship. The leverage comes from how you use your human capital and how well you convert some portion of your human capital to financial capital. It also includes your financial capital. These come together on the Life + Wealth Achievement Balance Sheet, which we'll look at in the next section.

AIM. When I talk about Aim, I'm focused on obtaining clarity around what you want, and developing the skills that go into the act of designing a plan. Your financial capital needs purpose. It can't work for you without it. So in Aim, we're doing the work of arriving at purpose.

Do you know people who seem to be busy all the time but don't move higher on the economic or life satisfaction meter? They're chasing the latest financial fad or following the prescription of rules of thumb they learned in a book and can't figure out why they're not getting results? It's because the action doesn't directly tie back to their aim. And this leads to the third A: Alignment.

ALIGNMENT. At its core, alignment is about ensuring you are building strategy. Think about what makes the difference between pros and amateurs in sports and in the performing arts. Amateurs may work hard but they don't have a strategy behind why they're doing it. Meanwhile, pros have a tight alignment between outcome and resources, which drives the specific action they take.

Alignment is effectively about controlling today for:

1. *Money.* Cash flows in and out in the present, but the present cash flows include those commitments made in the past and they also include an allocation to our future self. The question is how much to each?

2. *Time.* How do you allocate your time to all of the projects and activities in the areas of life you want to improve?

3. *Resources.* What's available to you and how can you best utilize them?

Alignment is about knowing what to do, and making decisions based on strategy rather than falling for the latest idea.

- Should you focus on debt payoff like all the books and blogs tell you?

- Should you focus on shifting at least 10% of take home wages into an investment before you do anything else, like many blogs, books and programs tell you to?

- Should you always buy instead of rent?

The alignment lever is about how well your decisions are tied to your best opportunities so that it sets you up to take the action that has the most impact to your future. This is where the ability to think strategically makes a big difference between selecting goals that become stepping-stones versus those that are keeping us busy.

ACTION. Is about how well you execute the projects needed to carry out the strategy.

- It is about your tax structuring.

- It is about your cash flow plan.

- It is about automating where you can.

- It is about clear direction for your financial capital.

- It is about building momentum through a lot of small wins.

ATTENTION. The last piece of this framework is attention. We need to measure and iterate. It's about asking questions that keep us on track to what's truly important to us as described via our work in 'Aim'. For example:

- How well are you converting your human capital to financial capital?

- What is your Quality of Life (QOL) Indicator saying?

- How well is your business or career supporting the development of your human and social capital?

For many people, measurement can be like fingernails on a chalkboard, but it's necessary. Professional athletes and top performers review their events and their stats, then they work with their coach on what needs to be adjusted — that's what got them to the professional level.

Seeing what the results are based on the actions you're taking, plus how your financial capital is working and closing those information loops provides increased confidence. This leads to increased competency and ultimately to direct control.

The mastery level of the *5A's* with *Life + Wealth Achievement Formula* is to be so dialed in to your own life that, if you make adjustments in one area, you know how all the other areas will react. It's about coordinating and integrating so that you can break through to a higher level of satisfaction and certainty in life and wealth.

Build Your Cross-Border Life + Wealth Achievement Plan™

If your cross-border financial plan is built without your direct collaborative involvement, you may end up with a slightly better financial planning process, but what you really need is something completely different. A *Cross-Border Life + Wealth Achievement Plan* is a model of how you expect (because you've designed it) your life to unfold. Only you know what you want your life to be, and you may not always be crystal clear on that, so you want the flexibility to change your mind.

We build out a *Cross-Border Life + Wealth Achievement Plan* using *Life + Wealth Achievement Formula and The 5 A's of Achievement*.

A *Cross-Border Life + Wealth Achievement Plan* is both ongoing and dynamic, so it helps with keeping the day-to-day moving, without feeling like you're stuck in tactical busywork without an overarching plan.

Imagine that it's December 31st. You're celebrating the twelve months that ended today. You're thinking about all that you're grateful for as you run through memories — highlights of the year that is coming to an end play like a movie trailer in your head. You think, *"I can't remember that last time I felt so at ease and confident, going into a new year"*.

You let your mind wander to the year that's about to start and you take a quick inventory of how you think life will go for you. That film reel runs in your head again. You have some key outcomes.

Now you're reflecting on the process you just completed. Your acknowledging all that you accomplished: First, you were able to look out to a third year and put some more clarity around key milestones. Maybe it's a family trip with parents for a vow renewal, or it's another move. The point is you know that those events are being handled, not in a way that feels like you are locked in to these goals, but in a way that feels good. Second, you shifted your attention to your longer-term plan to measure impact. Working from the longer term to the shorter term of your milestones, you thought about what more, if anything, needed to be added to the short-term specifics.

The idea here is simple: as one year of the rolling short-term plan ends, you add one at the longer end of the short-term plan. In this way, you are effectively "rolling forward" a year, allowing that year to come into focus now that you're a year closer to it. This allows for small and consistent course corrections. Thinking in a shorter time frame inspires us to act based on what is actually happening or what we want to happen versus what we think will happen.

Make no mistake. There is a difference between creating a "rolling short-term plan" and making short-term decisions that direct the longer-term plan by default. When you stay short term and keep allocating money and your financial capital based only on short-term views, it contributes to uncertainty. It results in a hodgepodge of financial structures and products purchased over the years from various professionals and salespeople based on the "going" wisdom of the time, and it results in a general imbalance among the personal, social, and financial aspects of life and wealth.

Think of your *Cross-Border Life + Wealth Achievement Plan* as a radar screen. As life events come into view, like weather patterns show up on radar images, we determine the level of attention these events deserve and then make adjustments to our plan as needed.

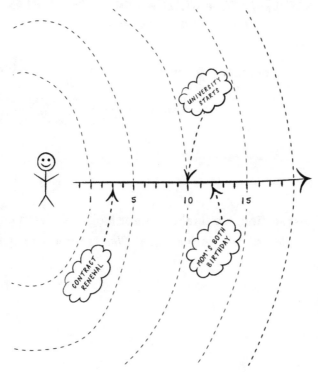

In the plan-building process, we determine the likely expenditures for the next twelve to twenty-four months. The primary focus is on what is happening in the coming twelve months but with a view toward the bigger picture twenty-four to thirty-six months out. The annual process thus updates the forecast out twelve to twenty-four months, but gives a view of the next year out thirty-six months. This way, each year's planning is never a cold start.

We build in flexibility by understanding that the exercise is not really the plan itself, meaning it isn't about producing a work of art to hang on a wall. It's about focusing our energy on the ongoing process of planning.

Here is an example of how a *Cross-Border Life + Wealth Achievement Plan* would look with plan review/updates every six months:

CROSS-BORDER LIFE + WEALTH ACHIEVEMENT PLAN WITH SCHEDULED PLAN UPDATES

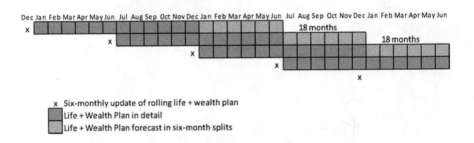

x Six-monthly update of rolling life + wealth plan
Life + Wealth Plan in detail
Life + Wealth Plan forecast in six-month splits

In the next section, we'll take a closer look at the elements of the *Cross-Border Life + Wealth Achievement Plan*, so you can get started building one.

SECTION TWO

BUILD YOUR CROSS-BORDER LIFE +
WEALTH ACHIEVEMENT PLAN

Much like the traditional SWOT analysis of business fame, your *Cross-Border Life + Wealth Achievement Plan* considers your strengths and what you already have working for you, along with the opportunities that exist in the context of the vision you have for your life and that of your family. It also considers challenges and issues as the specific jurisdictions are brought into the strategic planning process.

My goal for this section is to give you enough detail and guidance that you can apply this yourself.

Along our journey together, I'll mention resources that you can access on. This bonus material allows me to provide additional resources and details on selected topics.

To access the resources: go to <u>www.crossborderliving.com/book.</u>

4

INVENTORY YOUR ASSETS

The Life + Wealth Achievement Balance Sheet

A balance sheet is a financial picture of an individual or family at a point in time. Most personal finance books and advisors typically exclude the value of earning power from the balance sheet and thus do not convey an accurate financial picture.

The *Life + Wealth Achievement Balance Sheet* remedies this, allowing for the balance sheet to be a useful planning tool rather than a backward looking accounting exercise.

What is human capital?

Your human capital is made up of your education and knowledge, your skills and expertise, your experience and ideas. In short, what you earn in income is because of your skills and your effort.

My reason for showing human capital on the balance sheet is not to put more pressure on you. It's to remind you that *you have the power to shape your life*. So, the number we use is not to put you in a box, so to speak, nor is it to constrain you in any way. It's to show you— based on what we have to work with right now in the form of net earnings, assuming you do nothing to improve that situation— the present value of that income stream for the time period we have assumed it will continue.

Think of it this way: it's effectively the cumulative total of how we are providing value to the world, today (as represented by money, M, in the previous section), over a given time period; typically expected work years.

Technically, there are more aspects to the calculation, such as age—or the time until you plan to stop being able to, or choose to earn income—health, occupation, industry and experience among other factors, but the point here is to understand it conceptually.

Before we continue, I want to pause for a moment to show you a deliberately crude representation of how the components of wealth, looking only at human capital and financial capital, might shift, (e.g., how one might convert their human capital to financial capital and eventually start spending the capital versus the income it generates) over a lifetime.

The illustration below shows total wealth (the combination of human capital and financial capital on the *Life + Wealth Achievement Balance Sheet*) over time.

REPRESENTATION OF TOTAL WEALTH OVER TIME

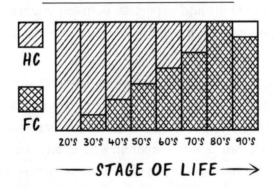

In the illustration, we see a 20-something person who has only human capital to work with. Over time, this person's human capital is shrinking as it is assuming no change in the earned income over increasingly shorter amounts of time, to the extended "stop working" age in the decade of the seventies. In our perfect world of illustrations, our person has managed to convert a sufficient amount of human capital to financial capital so that that the value of the financial capital exactly matches the original value of human capital, and by the end of their hypothetical lifetime have only spent down a fraction of their financial capital, leaving a larger percentage to be allocated according to their legacy goals.

A typical question here is: "What do I do if I don't like my number?" Well, that is a fantastic question! Congratulations for asking it!

Let me add some perspective: that number represents where you are in your career or your business right now, massaged by some assumptions. The question for you is, "what needs to happen in your career or your business for this number to change?"

When I first moved overseas I didn't work. I talked to potential employers and I (sort of) considered going into business for myself. I say "sort of" because truthfully I had this idea in my head that I was supposed to get a job. I was twenty-three and female. Yes, I had a degree in finance and I had passed the first of six educational exams that led to the CERTIFIED FINANCIAL PLANNER designation, but I had no work experience in personal financial planning and limited work experience in general outside of working in various departments of a U.S. regional bank since high school. Who would want to take advice from me? That was the type of business I would need to start; at least that's what I thought at the time. I didn't really have a lot of skills other than figure skating and I was living on a sub-tropical island, so not much there to work with.

In those early days my joint life and wealth balance sheet represented my husband's earnings projected out over a forty plus work horizon. And that was pretty much the only number on the asset side of the balance sheet. The only other number was the value of our joint checking account.

If I were in that position today, with the opportunities that technology has given us, I probably would have started Patterson

Partners in 1991 instead of 2005. Or at the very least, I would have considered it. Though I did have job offers during those very early days, they were from banks and I'd made a vow to myself that I would not put money ahead of me. Having worked for a bank and effectively having been mentored by senior bank employees, I knew in my heart that money would be my only motivation to accept such an offer. The other thing I could've done at the time, if I were in the same position today, is I could've put the specific knowledge and skills I obtained from my work experience (e.g., mortgage origination, mortgage servicing, accounting with accounts payable and accounts receivable, asset inventory for the branches, teller reconciliations) and/or the project management skills I obtained, by working on two capital asset projects, to work. I could also type quite well and I could merge documents because of my time in the word processing department. I could have worked remotely doing some of those things.

The decisions I made at that time affected the value that would be reflected on my joint life and wealth balance sheet with my husband. In some years my human capital number was zero, in other years my number was larger than my husband's number. It's not meant to be a static value.

As you can see in the drawing of the simplified *Life + Wealth Achievement Balance Sheet*, human capital is listed under the contingent assets group. A contingent asset represents the potential of something of economic value and that is dependent on future events to bring it to reality.

LIFE + WEALTH ACHIEVEMENT BALANCE SHEET

CASH/CASH EQUIVALENTS		*CURRENT LIABILITIES*	
CHECKING	20,000	CREDIT CARDS	10,000
SAVINGS	75,000		
		LONG-TERM LIABILITES	
INVESTMENT ASSETS		MORTGAGE	300,000
RETIREMENT PLANS	200,000		
INVESTMENT ACCTS	400,000	*TOTAL LIABILITIES*	
		HOME & CONTENTS	310,000
PERSONAL USE ASSETS			
HOME & CONTENTS	650,000	*NET WORTH*	2,735,000
CONTINGENT ASSETS			
HUMAN CAPITAL	1,700,000		
		TOTAL LIABILITIES	
TOTAL ASSETS	3,045,000	*AND NET WORTH*	3,045,000

In a globally mobile context, decisions are often made that directly affect our career. Human capital in the globally mobile world must be managed just as you would any other asset on a balance sheet.

The other usefulness of this number is that it provides some perspective for another part of the model: Plan Protection. The human capital number calculated the way I suggest shows us how much of our wealth is tied to a contingent asset. It also helps us visually understand the need to protect that asset against the risks of disability and death. I cover Plan Protection in more detail in Chapter 9.

Take a Money Inventory

Now that we've focused on the assets you have to work with, there are two more things you should know to create the results you want in your life: First, you should know what your lifestyle numbers look like. We do that using a tool called a *Money Inventory*. Second, to produce clarity, to improve communication between you and your partner, and to make more effective decisions as a couple, you must understand The 3 C's of Cash flow.

What is a Money Inventory?

You're probably familiar with the concept of inventory for business purposes: as a noun, inventory means a complete list of tangible goods or intangible qualities; the verb is the creation of the list itself. Sometimes the phrases "taking stock of" or "stock taking" are used. In our case, we're organizing and taking stock of routine living costs. You're not making any decisions as you conduct the inventory. So a money inventory is not a cash flow plan. In fact, it doesn't consider income at all; it's entirely focused on expenses.

The Money Inventory and the Worksheet will help you know what numbers you are working with as you develop strategy. It is set up in a way that provides a lot of insight.

A Money Inventory is a particularly valuable planning tool when you are considering relocation because it prompts you to obtain information specific to your needs, circumstances and wishes.

I often hear that people use a cost of living comparison calculator as a substitute for specific numbers — a shortcut of sorts. I address rules of thumb and other shortcuts later on in the book. My opinion here, is if you are comparing locations based on a fixed income amount in a fixed currency, a cost of living comparison can provide some useful context, but it's not a tool that will provide sufficient, specific information that will, in turn, ultimately assist you in making good decisions. The point of a cost of living comparison calculator is to *ensure parity of wages* across country borders.

To effectively conduct a Money Inventory, you must understand the 3 C's of Cash Flow.

The 3 C's of Cash Flow

This is all about the concepts of money past, money present and money future and the role they play in decision-making.

Effective cash design means being aware of any conflicts that exist between decisions we made in the past that affect the present, those things we want in the present and those things and situations we need to cover in the future. In short, your cash flow strategy has to match up money earned today with money it spends today, but that money we spend today is actually made up of a web of payments due for decisions made in the past, payments for things we need to cover in the present day and payments for things we want in the future. So, we're always seeking to find equilibrium between money past, money present, and money future when designing strategy.

Money Past is represented by the *Commitment Bucket, C1;*

Money Present is represented by the *Consumption Bucket, C2;* and

Money Future is represented by the *Coming Bucket, C3.*

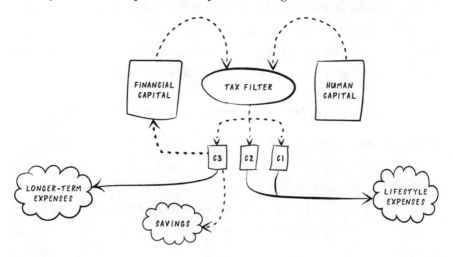

Chunking or grouping the expenses into these buckets helps visualize data and recognize patterns.

Money Past is the regular and fixed payments you have; for instance, your mortgage or rent, car payments, insurance, debt and taxes. For most people, these are going to be relatively fixed, meaning you can't easily change the amount that is due each month. Most of these will be in the Commitment Bucket. These are agreements or contracts you agreed to in the past or an expense you incurred in the past that have a current payment. Other examples are school fees, memberships like the gym or social clubs, child support and alimony, any pledges you made to charities or causes. Finally, if you are supporting your parents or any other family members, then include that figure in this bucket as well.

Money Present is money you need to cover typical day-to-day expenses like food. It also includes housing, utilities, clothing, out-of-pocket health care costs, transportation, gifts, professional fees, personal expenses. These types of expenses are grouped together in the Consumption Bucket.

Money Future is funds you allocate to achieve your short-term and long-term goals. At this point in the process, you have not set any goals, so for now, you would only allocate an amount to a goal that already exists and for which you have already determined a savings figure and frequency (e.g. USD 500 per month).

There are 5 Steps to Complete a Money Inventory

Download a Money Inventory Worksheet from the resources page, which you can access once you register at www.crossborderliving.com/book. Once you have the Money Inventory Worksheet, follow the 5 steps to complete it. Remember, you'll want to conduct a money inventory for each currency or country.

Step 1. Enter the typical or average amount you spend for each of the sub-categories by frequency.

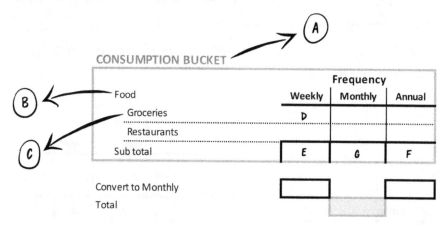

Within each Money Bucket (A) there are categories (B) and subcategories (C).

For each subcategory, you will want to think about if you typically spend money in the subcategory. If you do, then think about how often this takes place and how much you spend.

In the illustration, we can see that area D is where we'd write the number that represents the typical amount we spend on groceries on a weekly basis. We are entering the figure in the weekly column because that most closely represents the frequency of the activity. We would not fill in the other columns for that subcategory because we don't shop for groceries only once every so often each year.

Step 2. Subtotal the categories by frequency.

Total all of the weekly amounts (E), the annual amounts (F) and the monthly amounts (G).

Step 3. Convert all subtotals to a monthly total.

For the weekly column, you will be multiplying the figure (E) by 52, and then dividing by 12. Place this total in E1.

For the annual column, you will divide the subtotal in F by 12 and place that total in F1.

CONSUMPTION BUCKET

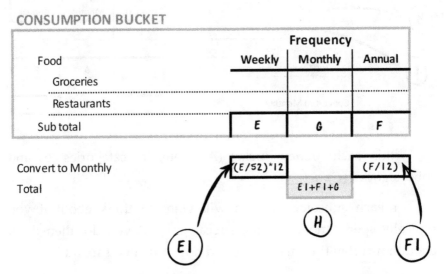

	Frequency		
Food	**Weekly**	**Monthly**	**Annual**
Groceries			
Restaurants			
Sub total	E	G	F

Convert to Monthly: (E/52)*12 , (F/12)

Total: E1+F1+G

H

E1   F1

To obtain the total monthly amount, you will add the amounts in E1 and F1 to the total in G and place that in H.

Step 4. Allocate totals according to how these expenses are handled right now.

For the money inventory, there are only three ways these expenses are handled: they are paid out of some kind of household account, which is most likely jointly owned HH); they are paid out of an account owned separately by either you (IN1) or your partner (IN2).

CONSUMPTION BUCKET

Food	Frequency			Who & How Much?		
	Weekly	Monthly	Annual	HH	IND1	IND2
Groceries	300			1,300		
Restaurants		950		400	200	350
Sub total	300	950	-	1,700	200	350

Convert to Monthly	1300	-
Total	2,250	

The illustration shows a total of 2,250 in outflows for food during a typical month. The outflows can be specifically seen as groceries being paid out of a household account in the entirety. We also see that restaurants are handled differently, with an amount that each individual typically covers on their own or out of an account in their sole names, while another amount is allocated for the household.

This exercise is particularly insightful for sole proprietors and business owners. If you spend family money on things like business lunches, allocate them here, but add some notes that you can refer to in later steps of the overall process. We want to be sure that, ultimately, you are separating business expenses from personal expenses.

Two common questions arise here. To address one of them, I should clarify the role of the Coming Bucket for Money Inventory purposes. The Money Inventory is an inventory of expenses taking place now or expected to take place in the coming twelve months. In the alignment phase of this process, the Inventory will hit reality; so don't think of this as anything other than a preliminary run at numbers. It's a baseline from which we can make adjustments. If you are already moving money from a household account or any individual accounts to some kind of short or long-term savings, then inventory it. If you are making that a "non-negotiable" for the coming twelve months, then inventory it. Otherwise, leave that section blank.

The second question goes something like this: "I don't track my expenses, how do I take a money inventory?" This is not about proving that we have any bookkeeping or accounting skills. I don't track my household's expenses, although I will look them up when I conduct a Money Inventory. The reason I don't track per se is because I know where the money should be going. Think about it. Do you really think it's a good idea to know where your money goes *after the fact*? That would freak me out because it would mean I have no idea, and thus no control, over my money.

Let's take a minute or two to talk about using last year's expenses, whether from bank statements, credit card bills or any data storage device.

I suggest you first attempt a Money Inventory without referring back to any of last year's numbers. If you have no idea what your key family members expect to spend on a category, ask them. Be sure to first ask them how often they spend money on the category, and then ask how much they spend on average.

Looking back at bills and looking through account statements is fine. What I don't want you to do is to get caught up in reconciling last year's bank statements and entering them into personal accounting software. You aren't going to finish this project in a timely manner and we need you to keep moving forward. If you think you can't remember how much you spent on electricity last month, then by all means have a look, but here's the thing. I need you to think about that a bit deeper. Staying with the subcategory of electricity, think about the season you're in right now and how the season is affecting the bill. For example, if it is winter right now and you have electric heating then think a minute about usage in the summer. Will your usage be higher or lower? Also, this is another common challenge: If any of your goals for this year include a renovation, consider if you are going to see a spike in electricity for a couple of months. Are you replacing less efficient appliances with more efficient ones? Are you adding more appliances or maybe an electric pool pump? That will definitely add to your electricity bill. Take the higher number as your average monthly cost of electricity and write that on the money inventory sheet. That thought process is what is important here. It's more important than taking an old number and just assuming that is the correct number going forward. The Money Inventory is a planning tool, not an accounting tool. Planning looks forward, accounting looks backward to tell you what's already happened.

If you really have no idea where the money is going, this insight is useful. Do your best on the Money Inventory worksheet and move forward in the process.

Now that you have an idea of how wealth is created, you know that you can make a difference, and an income at the same time, by sharing your skills, your advice, *and* your life story with others and you've quantified your regular living expenses, it's time to start designing.

5

LIFE DESIGN

We are always getting ready to live but never living.
— Ralph Waldo Emerson

One of the biggest mistakes people make when creating a financial plan is the assumption that they can breeze through this part of the process. I see this with clients I work with all the time. They think that because they've filled out questionnaires and have set some goals they can move on to the more "complicated" areas or the areas where they have most interest. But that's not always the case. Many times in the goal planning stage we think we know what we want, or we don't want to take the time to really think about what we really want, how things are really going. But this costs us a lot more in the long run. Let's take a closer look at this.

The Complicated Stuff

Money is often cited as one of the major contributors to the breakdown of marriage. Many of us know this to be true. Below are a few anecdotes from cross-border families struggling to come to terms with money issues after relocating overseas. They are excerpted from "Family Matters!" Report on the Key Findings of the ExpatExpert.com/AMJ Campbell International Relocation Survey, 2008[10]:

"Our family grew apart at first...and are now back to good. The reason we grew apart is definitely over finances. I felt isolated and missed my friends and resentful that we felt 'broke' and it appeared to be on me to get a job — when there were so many things we

---

[10] "Family Matters!" Report on the Key Findings of the ExpatExpert.com/AMJ Campbell International Relocation Survey, 2008

needed to do that required me to be at home (nothing is open late or on weekends in Europe for the most part). In addition, we had tension building between us with the lack of information from the company on our living and financial arrangements before we moved... And, we had a really healthy and strong marriage for a long time before the relocation."

"We fought quite a bit about our finances and how some of the relocation support allowances were not enough to make up for my pay decrease due to relocation. We also fight about children's education quite a bit as they are not currently in top schools, which also lack after-school activities."

However, in my experience and in at least one study, "For Richer, For Poorer: Money as a Topic of Marital Conflict in the Home" by Lauren M. Papp, Ph.D; E. Mark Cummings, Ph.D. and Marcie C. Goeke-Morey, Ph.D.[11] money is very often a symptom of other issues. The real source of conflict is a lack of alignment or agreement on how the money may be used — the money is just the tool. The conflict is because of a different reason.

The complications arise because of our differing cultural and familial imprints, our identity, and our priorities. Because we don't have a model of how to reconcile all these things we do the best we can, but not without conflict.

In this chapter I'm going to walk you through the process of identifying your needs and goals, communicating that to your partner and working through it to best accommodate each other's' personal, familial and financial needs and priorities.

---

[11] Papp Ph.D., Lauren M, E. Mark Cummings Ph.D., and Marcie C. Goeke-Morey, Ph.D., "For Richer, For Poorer: Money as a Topic of Marital Conflict in the Home." *Fam Relat.* 2009 February; National Institute of Heath, Sept 2017
https://www.ncbi.nlm.nih.gov/pmc/articles/PMC3230928/pdf/nihms335530.pdf

We all have a vision or goal for our life. It might not be completely clear, but everyone wants to live an extraordinary life, where we live, work, play and make a difference; a life where we are moving with momentum toward the things that matter to us. In a cross-border life, we want to feel like our relationships and cultural skills have gotten to a level where we're confident in social situations and have influence in getting others to support us in our dreams, or to help us make a big difference in other people's lives. But we often struggle with clarifying our vision and desires. Sometimes it's because we aren't fully aware of our surroundings.

The 3 D's of Life and Lifestyle

After twenty-five years of working with private clients, fifteen years of financial and life coaching, and studying different aspects of psychology, I've noticed that people tend to *live one of three types of life and lifestyle*: Default, Decent and Designed. We are all in one of those three lives today, and we can choose to keep it, adjust it, or change it altogether.

THE 3 D'S OF LIFE AND LIFESTYLE

DEFAULT ⟶ DECENT ⟶ DESIGNED

The Default Life

Many people live their lives in the past or in the expectations of others. Aspects of this life can be traced to cultural or familial imprints. Because they've let other people or the past dictate who they are their identities are trapped in a set of beliefs about what is possible. Their experience in life — their thoughts, feelings and behaviors are restricted. They may feel tethered to where they are or cornered into a certain way of being, complete with labels, assumptions, and expectations that may be false. If we feel like we cannot leave this life, we may feel resentment to the causes of this life.

From birth, we are enticed with rewards and punishment to do what others — our parents, teachers, employers, friends, lovers, bosses, clients, customers and even society and our government — want us to do. The end result is that we adapt and assimilate so much that our actions and desires start to fall in line with external rewards. Over time, we accept this into our routines and reality. It can become a lens through which we see the world and as long as we are receive the rewards — attention, money, and care for example — being in this life has a lot going for it. At some point in our lives we have all probably lived this life and because of it we may have felt controlled or locked-in, restless to leave. Some people refer to this existence as a cage. Some of us find our way out when something happens that shows us the reality of the life we're living and the life we *could* have. We then break the cage and *consciously* choose a new self-image and life and do the (sometimes hard) work of sculpting it into reality.

The Decent Life

For many of us, life is not as dire as the Default life. Through work, dedication and fortunate circumstances, many of us live what I call the Decent life. We've followed a similar path to independence, opportunity, and some level of freedom. We have spouses or partners, one or more kids or causes, or both. We may have real estate in the form of a personal residence and possibly a rental property or two. We are thankful for our lives. We know we've made some tradeoffs — a few more hours at the office away from the family, or we've put the career on hold to raise the family, or perhaps we've opted for a less adventurous life — but we knew what we were getting into...for the most part. Then one day, you reply to the question of how things are going in your life with a crafted upbeat answer but in the back of your mind you start to wonder if you're being totally honest. Are you happy or have you made too many trade-offs? Is this the life you dreamed of and the goals you wanted to achieve? Are you more fun than the life you're living? You have a degree (or two) hanging on the wall (or in storage) but you aren't utilizing any of the skills you've obtained by getting it? Is this what you really wanted? Are you living your life or someone else's? Often our brain responds to these types of questions with guilt.

Although this is not the same type of cage as the Default life, we can start to feel trapped in the Decent life. Although this may be a comfortable life, we can start to feel restless and wonder: *How did I end up here?*

While the Default life feels scary and limited by external conditions, the Decent life can feel stale and limited by its own success. There is a similarity between these two lives: It is a desire for something more. More freedom, more choice, parity, connection, authenticity. Fill in the blank. Ultimately what is missing from both is a life of our design.

The Designed Life

In the Designed life, we create our own world. We're not in cruise control. We're on a journey, focusing attention where we want it focused for the life we want to live. This doesn't mean perfect balance in each area of life, but it does mean being deliberate about where we focus our time and energy. This also means focusing the money we earn from focusing our time and energy helping others in a way that best supports and inspires us.

It might seem like the Designed life is a destination, one where those living it have no obstacles or challenges. But that would be a misunderstanding. When we're designing, we understand that we, and thus our life, are a work in progress. We still have highs and lows, but overall, we take the time to check in, to reflect, to vision, to create goals and plans to achieve those goals and we adjust as needed.

The Designed life usually calls to us after we've done what we were supposed to do, become who we thought we were supposed to become, and lived as we thought we were supposed to live.

"Congratulations! You are only a few years away from retirement," said the benefits seminar leader. *Congratulations?* Mark thought. *Retirement means more decisions about more things I can't control.* As the presentation progressed, Mark's thoughts drifted off to questions and fears. *The decisions that I make now will dictate my lifestyle for the rest of my life. How long could I live on my savings? What am I going to do after I retire? Am I really ready to stop working? Where am I going to live? Will my money support me if I don't work full or part time? Ugh this is too stressful.*

Can you relate to what Mark's thinking?

As the internationally mobile leader or co-leader of your family, the odds are that your career is largely responsible for your current circle of friends, your financial well-being, the location of your current home, aspects of your leisure and recreation, and possibly your community and social relationships. In short, whether you realize it or not, your career or your spouse's career, has probably been central to your life decisions. Like many, you may have been or still may be immersed in your work. There are lists of things to do and goals to achieve. You may pride yourself on doing these things well. It's tough to imagine that your peers or company can survive without you. The questions that Mark is contemplating relate to how to fill the space in the period of time post your prime career. The answers to these questions (and others) can determine whether this period of life will be an exciting new time in your life or a dark and dreary one.

Research has found a drastic difference between the non-retired individual's concerns about retirement and the *actual* disappointments faced by the retiree. Prospective retirees list their biggest concerns as poor health and financial worries; however, actual retirees rated alienation as the biggest disappointment, followed by health. By alienation, they are referring to being lonely and cut off from former colleagues, groups and organizations and feeling behind the times. Many also miss the satisfaction they received from performing their job and having a day-to-day routine and goals. This is particularly an issue for those who have moved away from their nuclear family to live abroad either temporarily or permanently.

Because choices made today impact our future, it's important to seek growth and development in all areas of life throughout adulthood. The *Life + Wealth Compass* and the exercises that go with it, are important life planning tools. Those who incorporate The *Life + Wealth Compass* into their life-planning, will likely find the phase of life that follows retirement and/or repatriation to be a rich and rewarding experience. That is because, along the way, they have been preparing for a full life, and not only preparing for that event. Mark's best plan for retirement will be comprehensive — a blueprint for life that allocates all of his personal resources: time, energy, skills and money that are most meaningful to him as an individual. You can have that too.

The key conversation for you to have centers on what the life you would design for yourself looks like. Then you must find the strength to step out of your comfort zone to identify things that need to change to start you on the path of transformation to that life.

We start the journey with a compass.

The *Life + Wealth Compass* — A Marker to Aid in Finding Your Bearing

A compass helps you determine your position on a map and keeps you headed in the direction of your destination. If you change course or encounter obstacles that might not show on the map, a compass can help guide you to your destination.

The *Life + Wealth Compass* is a tool that can be used to assess the *8 Facets of Daily Living*[12]

THE 8 FACETS OF DAILY LIVING

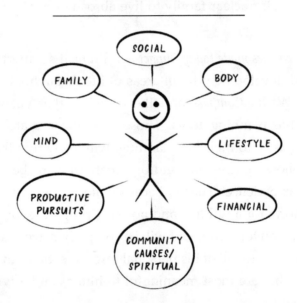

Social includes spending time with at least one friend, new social relationships you would like to build, time with best friends, cultivating relationships with like-minded people, organizations to expand your relationships, relationships you would like to expand, limit or eliminate.

---

[12] The Life & Wealth Compass and the Facets of Daily Living are adapted from the "Wheel of Life" Copyright ©, Money Quotient, Inc. Adapted and used by permission of Money Quotient, Inc.

Community & Causes/Spirituality are activities you participate in or support that have an impact on societies, groups or causes, as well as living your religious beliefs, reading books on spirituality, meditation, finding and pursuing your unique gifts and purpose.

Mind includes activities and educational opportunities that increase understanding, knowledge, skills and mental acuity and enhance your career. It also includes activities that involve meaningful work, your money attitudes and beliefs, and the exhibition of positive money behavior.

Lifestyle includes activities for personal enjoyment and for refreshing the body, mind and spirit; the type and location of housing and whether you want a mobile lifestyle or want to settle in one place; general travel and adventure; luxuries; and what you do with your time.

Body includes your health and nutrition, personal care, and general vitality.

Family relates to your inner circle of immediate family, close relationships, and extended family, if you wish.

Productive Pursuits is about your human capital, whether it results in the exchange of money or not. For instance: your career(s), your business(es), part-time consulting, lecturing and teaching whether paid or not.

Financial includes any overall financial goals or wishes that don't fit anywhere else. It can include how well your career or business supports your life, the amount of debt you carry, protection against catastrophic events such as death, disability, job loss, or environmental disasters, and your relationships with various financial advisors. It also covers cash flow and how well that is working.

Take a Life Inventory

> "You can run after satisfaction, but satisfaction must come from within."

We're going to use the Life + Wealth Compass to help us take a personal inventory. In the first phase of designing we need some insight. Athletes look at game videos and track all their training routines. Actors and speakers look at films and presentations. If we want our lives to perform on a next level; we should adopt the same strategy.

Taking a life inventory helps provide clarity of where we are right now in all the different areas of life, specifically the *8 Facets of Daily Living*. We're going to look at one of the facets here, but to get the most out of this step, I encourage you to download the *Life + Wealth Compass Worksheet* from the book resources vault and complete this exercise for all of the Facets of Daily Living.

We're going to use *Family* as an example. Here we're focused on your relationship with your partner, your children, and if you want your extended family. I'd like you to think about how satisfied you are in this area and rate it.

Family Facet of Daily Living

On a scale from 1 to 10, how satisfied are you in this area right now?

Poor	Fair	Good	Very Good	Excellent
1 2	3 4	5 6	7 8	9 10

Score: _____

Now, write out why you rated this category the way you did. What is happening now that indicates this score? There are no right or wrong answers here. Describe what this rating looks and feels like to you.

Why did you rate your level of satisfaction this way?

_____

_____

_____

Next, write down what needs to happen, generally — no specific time frame here — to improve your score. This could be a list or you could write a paragraph. Just jot down what comes to mind immediately without editing.

What must happen to improve the rating?

_____

_____

_____

Now that you know what needs to happen to improve this area and you know how you feel about it, it's time to decide if the change you have identified is something you want to take action on. Is it an area that you want to mark off as an area of focus for the next twelve months (or longer if needed)?

This may just seem like a step in a process, but don't underestimate the power here. *If you don't consciously choose what you want to focus on*, your brain will do it for you and choose what it usually focuses on. Change requires time and energy. Make an active choice.

Choose. Is this a key area of focus for your integrated life and wealth map for the next twelve months?   Yes   No

Repeat for all of the *8 Facets of Daily Living* using the worksheet in our book resource area.

Once you've your completed worksheet, you'll use it to continue your inventory, think of the areas where you feel you are on course and why you believe they're on course. Then consider, if you maintain this course in these areas how does your life and wealth looks in your mind's eye five years from now? Five years, to ten years from now? Assuming you maintain the current course, how does that specific area look? How will your overall life and wealth look? Next, rate your satisfaction in your life and wealth, and in that Facet of Life, ten years from now. Skip this step and you may not even realize that you're off course until too much time has passed and your life is harder to reset.

Refer back to the 8 Facets of Daily Living to help you complete the following questions.

1. In what areas do you feel you are on the right course? Why?

2. If you maintain your current course (or status quo) in these areas of life and wealth, what will your sense of satisfaction likely be in five years? In ten years?

_____

_____

_____

_____

_____

With this insight, finalize your inventory, think about any areas where you want to change course and note them. Think about and write down why you want to make changes here and why it's important.

Vision

Once you've taken an inventory of what has worked so far, and what hasn't and you've gathered some ideas about what could change or improve going forward, you'll need to shift focus to imagine the person you want to be and the life you want to live or have wanted to live. It's in this step that we want to challenge your limiting beliefs and give voice to your dreams.

Keep in mind: There is no need to put limitations on what's possible. Of course, that doesn't mean throwing common sense out the door. If you have limited dance training, there may be little hope of a career as a prima ballerina. If you focus on something like this, you'll be diverting your energy away from where it can be most effective. But, when viewed intelligently there are no limits to the outcomes available to you. After all, limited goals create limited lives. So, stretch yourself as far as you want. I encourage you to write down what you really want because that's the only way you can expect to get it.

The word vision itself can be a challenge to many of us, because we automatically think we need to come up with a crystal clear picture of what we want to have one, three, or five years from now. But if we don't think visually, the process can be a hard one.

At the end of the day, our vision is the imaginary thing pulling us forward. It can be fueled by something inspiring or it can be fueled initially by something perceived as negative. I remember being inspired to create a compelling vision that included returning to my high school one day as a successful professional. This came about because an administrator told me that because of who my father was, I would never amount to anything so I shouldn't bother taking "advanced level" courses. That negative feedback prompted me to bigger and better goals; ones that I might not have aspired to.

Visualization is a very important step in the planning process. It can act as a mental rehearsal—a way to sample or try out many lifestyle choices prior to making any commitments.

Frederic Hudson, Ph.D., an expert in the area of work/life balance and the author *of The Handbook of Coaching: A Comprehensive Resource Guide for Managers, Executives, Consultants, and Human Resource Professionals, explains*: "... What is the future? Not something waiting for you but something you create through your imagination. The future is possibility waiting for form, the 'not yet' waiting to be programmed."

If you're just starting out with this system and you don't yet have a strong and powerful vision for your life, that's okay. It'll come. As my yoga instructor likes to say, "use what's available to you right now."

The key here is not to get caught up in the concreteness of Vision. Vision has nothing to do with being concrete. It has everything to do with suspending disbelief, wondering what the future could hold and articulating that possibility. This could be your great aspiration for how your life will be better in some way. As you define your vision, shoot for clarity and focus as much as you can. For example, if you see yourself operating from anywhere in the world, serving more specialized types of customers, or experimenting with different products or services, write it all down. A key part of creating that vision is to ensure it's clear, whatever it might be.

"A goal is created three times. First as a mental picture. Second, when written down to add clarity and dimension. And third, when you take action towards its achievement."

- Gary Ryan Blair

Consider Living Part of Your Retirement Dream Today

Take Jane, for example, who turned sixty-five this year. She started transitioning into a life of her own design about seven years ago. She didn't want to stop working because working provided more than a paycheck — it provided several things that were important to her — a way to meet new people and explore new interests, to keep active physically and mentally, and for personal development. The trick; however, was determining what type of career would support the life that she desired. She found it — a complete change from her previous career — another industry, in fact. Along the way, her financial planning has shifted to support this new life. Many decisions were made, including paying off a mortgage early through accumulated savings and money received via a small inheritance. She also conducted a regular review of her mix of personal investments to be sure they were performing in line with expectations, continued to match her goals, and were relevant for the changing economic environment worldwide. While her life is not extravagant, Jane is able to travel to destinations such as Europe, Australia and New Zealand several times each year. Exploring is important to her and her life reflects that importance. Jane wasn't afraid to look inward and commit to making the necessary changes to arrive at a life of her design versus a life by default despite being both divorced and widowed during her life.

Jane represents the new model for life and wealth.

Imagine the life you want and then continue to build on it. The sharper and clearer your vision becomes, the more it will guide and direct the decisions you make and the actions you take on a short-term basis. This is a great way to adopt a "future focus" that will guide you to a life that you've designed for yourself (and perhaps for your family as well).

So, let's get started! In the next section, I'll walk you through how this all comes together.

If you remember, I asked you to choose which of the *8 Facets of Daily Living* you wanted to designate as a focus area. Once you have that, you want to create a vision for each of them. In fact, you will create two versions of your vision for that area of your life. I know it seems like overkill. But stay with me while I explain why below.

Create a Range of View

As we discussed, the most powerful visions address and align your dreams. But, when we start to envision a significant accomplishment—something that might be well beyond what we've achieved in the past — the question that most of us ask is "how can I actually do this?" and we start editing. This is the wrong question at this point in this system because you don't know how to do it. If you did, you'd likely already be doing it and living that reality.

I created the concept of the *range of view* to allow that big vision to exist on paper as one possibility rather than edit it down. I call it the ideal scenario. Sometimes we're not super clear about what we want but we are clear about what we *don't* want. At the other end of the range, then is what has to happen, the bare minimum. I call this the *minimally acceptable scenario.*

THE RANGE OF VIEW

This is what I love most about creating a "range of view": we've effectively created some descriptions of milestones on the path from where we are now to the ideal situation. So by describing the ideal and the minimally acceptable, we can mark out what this Facet of Daily Living looks like at different points in the range, which could be milestones or the vision you are going for. I'll cover that in more detail in a minute.

For now, you want to describe, in as much detail as possible, what the ideal for each of your chosen Facets of Life looks like to you. Write in the present tense so that if you read that description again you'll be able to clearly identify whether you met it or not. Engage all of your senses to describe the results you want for this Facet of Life. What will you see and hear? How does this benefit you? How does this vision benefit others? Repeat for the minimally acceptable version. Then, repeat for each of the Facets of Daily Living.

If you haven't done so already, you can download a *Life + Wealth Design Worksheet* at www.crossborderliving.com/book.

This is the point in the process where I encourage couples to share their designs with each other. This includes sharing the areas where you would like to focus, plus your ideas of how they look, from both an ideal and minimally acceptable point of view.

This is not about selling your ideas to your partner, it's about starting a conversation and discovering where each of you have overlap and where you don't.

IDEAS AND VISION → ALIGNMENT

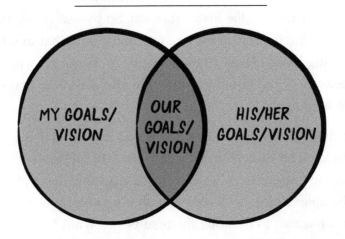

To clarify, we're not yet setting goals, *although the vision can become the goal.* You're considering the options together and considering the future version of each of you. If one or more areas allow you to create a joint vision for that area, then do so.

Once you've thought this through for one of the *8 Facets of Daily Living,* you'll choose the vision you want to adopt. This is where that range of view can come in handy and save some time. You may find that you want to adopt the ideal version or something else. The idea here is to come to a decision that works for both of you and *why* this version of your vision must happen.

You may find that the process of writing out the reasons that this vision needs in order to achieve it helps you further align on the topic area. If it doesn't align, then it will help you identify and work through any overlap and the areas where you may want to allow each other some freedom. I'm not a counselor so if you find this particularly difficult and you find that you really need some external help, I highly recommend you seek that out.

This process can also help you edit the vision. I've found that it's best to edit as much as needed so you both have the vision for this facet of life and why it must happen.

Once that is complete, think through and list the things that must happen to achieve the vision you have for this *Facet of Daily Living*. Be sure to assign a time frame and your best estimate of the costs associated with those outcomes. For example, if an outcome is dependent on your use of a professional, such as a personal trainer, a nutritionist, childcare, etc., list the cost(s) associated with what is needed to achieve that outcome. If you're not sure of the cost, research for the best estimate.

Choose up to three outcomes. We are shifting now into goal setting in this designing process, so I recommend that you limit the outcomes to no more than three. These outcomes are ideally all to be the milestones that get you to the vision within twelve months. This step is then repeated for each of the *8 Facets of Daily Living* that are the agreed focus areas.

> *"Knowing is not enough; we must apply.*
> *Willing is not enough; we must do."*
> — Johann Wolfgang Von Goethe

The Destination — A Vision of Your Overall Life

The idea behind all of the work I just outlined is to help you get clarity on what you want out of your life in the short term. However, we're still designing for the long term. It's like building your dream home from scratch. If you were designing a house, you'd now have specific ideas about how you want certain elements, like maybe your kitchen, to look and feel. How it might influence the traffic flow in that part of the house and why that appeals to you. Once you have clarity on all those aspects, a designer can usually come up with a visual representation for you of the entire house, so you can see how it all comes together.

When we are designing your life we follow a similar process. We want to create the vision for our life a year from now. If you can see beyond the end of twelve months, then jot that down as well.

The exercise in this step is to imagine that you've been pulled into an alternate reality. It's one year from tomorrow and you are having a conversation with your future self. What does the future you tell you about what happened over the past year? Why is he or she excited?

Use the space here or write in a journal.

If you wrote down any ideas for your life beyond twelve months, they may come in handy in this next step. Let's forecast this life three years from now and then answer the question about what you are most proud of.

What are three things you'll be proud of three years from now?

1. _____

2. _____

3. _____

This work is truly a large chunk of your life + wealth plan and a typically undervalued part. But I can honestly say that the money aspect of the designing stage that we will shift into, works out with more certainty and less stress when it knows what you want it to do for you. This work and the next steps are the key to making that happen.

Goal Setting

"There is no greater guarantee of a long, happy, healthy and prosperous life than for you to be continually working on being, having and achieving more and more of the things you really want. Clear goals enable you to release your full potential for personal and professional success. Goals enable you to overcome any obstacle and to make your future achievement unlimited."

— Brian Tracy

In the last section you identified outcomes and a vision for your life over a three-year period. To actually achieve these outcomes you must convert them into compelling goals. This turns the visions from aspirations to a motivating target that you can take specific actions to achieve.

Identify Your Top 10 Goals

Finally! So much more than decisions from a generic checklist, you're in the final step of designing — identifying the goals that you want to achieve that get you closer to the vision you have started to articulate for your life three years from now, and those specific goals for the next twelve months that you need to hit to make the vision for your life for *this* year come true.

Using the vision as a guide, you're going to look through all the outcomes you listed for the different facets of life and narrow them down to the one to ten outcomes you believe will get you to your vision. Think of these as the projects that need to be managed and met that get you to the life you want.

It's like building a house. Once we know what it's supposed to look like, and what we need—like a foundation, a roof, plumbing and all the contractors to make it happen—it's time to create a timeline.

	Category	I/MA	What will you specifically obtain or achieve?	By what date?
1.				
2.				
3.				
4.				
5.				
6.				
7.				
8.				
9.				
10.				

Balance Check

After you've made a first run at the top one-to-ten outcomes you want to achieve this year, take a minute to do a balance check. The idea here is to ask how well the goals you listed represent each area of your life. If you listed them by category, notice whether or not any one category is dominating. Is there a reasonable level of balance in your life represented here? We're not looking for perfection here, so it's okay if some areas receive more attention than others. Just be clear that you are designing your life in this way.

Your goals are the roadmap directing your life. Before we get too far in the map creation process and start integrating it with your money, take a moment to think about what your map looks like on a daily basis. Are you focusing exclusively on one area at the sacrifice of other areas?

> *"A goal is a planned conflict with the status quo."*
> — Hyrum W. Smith

It's important to know that this work is a step in the process. The zealous student may want to take goal setting to a level of detailed project management. You may have heard the saying no *plan survives first contact with reality*. We're going to look at aligning soon and in that step is where goals must survive reality but first let's look at another key element of the *Life + Wealth Map* – the tax filter.

6

UNDERSTAND YOUR TAX FILTER

At this point, three questions apply in developing your *Cross-Border Life + Wealth Achievement Plan*:

1. What countries, regions or municipalities are relevant?

2. How are they relevant?

3. Can a tax treaty help?

Before we get into that let's take a moment to talk about tax planning.

What is Tax Planning?

Tax planning is effectively creating a strategy to manage tax as a result of understanding the answers to the three questions above. Once we know the answers to the three questions, we can look for deductions, we can look to see if we can defer tax, we can determine if we can convert income from one type of income to another type (that is take income from capital gains instead of dividends etc.), and we can determine if tax elimination through credits and non-taxable income is possible. That's a general overview. I am not covering in detail how to create tax strategy here. That is a book in itself and I want to stay focused on covering key basics and providing an overview.

Let's talk about money flow for some context on why we need to understand our tax filter.

If you remember from the overview of *Life + Wealth Achievement Formula* we create money, M, from deploying our human capital, HC. Some of that money is used to support our core living expenses, C1 and C2, while some of that is diverted to the future (C3) to cover short- and mid-term expenses as well as savings, S. Savings (S), is then converted to financial assets or financial capital, FC, invested for financial independence and other longer term financial goals.

$$M = HC + E;$$

$$NEI = (M - T)$$

NEI is thus allocated across and therefore is equal to
$$(C1 + C2 + C3);$$

$$C3 = (STE + S);$$

$$FC = S + \textit{Life} + \textit{Wealth Investing}$$

Our financial capital, FC, also produces income, M, in the form of dividends, interest, capital gains and capital losses. The income is often going to be received in various currencies. All of this income will therefore also be subject to the tax filter, whether you see it or not, and whether it is reported to you from a custodian or not. This flow of income from both Human Capital and Financial Capital flowing through the Tax Filter to produce Net Earned Income is illustrated below. The illustration also shows the flow of this income across the 3 C's of Cash Flow, a portion of which is saved and ultimately converted to Financial Capital, and a portion of which is reinvested into the Financial Capital from which it was produced.

THE FLOW OF INCOME THROUGH THE TAX FILTER AND ACROSS THE 3 C'S OF CASH FLOW

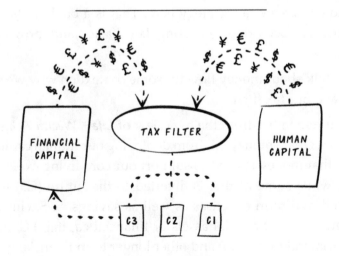

Why is This Important?

In short, tax can be legally minimized by understanding the rules. Let's consider a common situation that can be avoided by simply understanding how it all works: Let's use Peter as an example. Peter is a non-U.S. citizen and non-resident of the United States. He has an investment account that he owns solely with a U.S. broker-dealer (e.g. an online trading account). If we look at the account statement we see (in simple non-detailed terms) a mix of U.S. based investments and some common shares of non-U.S. companies. Because of the rules that apply to him, the interest and dividend income from the U.S. based equity holdings is going to be subject to a tax withholding of 30%. Imagine that statement in your mind. We see $1,000 in dividend income from U.S. investments and then we see later in the statement that cash is reduced by a total of $300. We also see the sale of one U.S. asset, and after looking a bit closer we realize there is a capital gain resulting from the sale of that item. We don't see any withholding tax. That is because the U.S. does not tax capital gains on this particular type of investment for non-resident, non-citizens. We look again at the statement and see that there is also a dividend from one of the non-U.S. companies that Peter owns in this account. We see the letters FTW and money being deducted from cash. That is the tax withholding due to the other government. The amount will be determined based on the rules that apply given the situation.

But how do we know the rules to apply? We'll know by answering the questions below:

1. What countries, regions or municipalities are relevant?

How Residency, Citizenship/Nationality and Domicile Affect Your Cross-Border Financial Matters and Plans

The world is comprised of nearly two hundred independent states and a sprinkling of dependent jurisdictions, each with the authority to collect tax in its territory. In addition, many of these independent nations have territories within their country borders that also have the authority to levy tax. Few of the nearly two hundred sovereign states and their internal authorities apply an identical tax regime. Not only does the definition and type of tax vary among these jurisdictions, but the policies underlying the tax systems vary as well. The problem for international families is the possibility of double or excessive taxation.

A liability or tax often arises due to the concept of a connecting factor, also known as nexus.

A connecting factor may be derived from a personal attachment, such as nationality, domicile or residence, for an individual. A legal entity such as a corporation may have a connecting factor as a result of its place of incorporation or place of central management and control. Last, economic connection might exist if there is activity conducted in a jurisdiction that is income generating, or if an asset is located in that jurisdiction.

To understand how this applies to your situation we need to look at each connecting factor in more detail:

Personal Attachment

The first objective in cross-border financial planning is to determine the extent to which a person is subject to tax in a given jurisdiction both during their lifetime and upon death.

Citizenship/Nationality

Citizenship or nationality is the primary connecting point for many aspects of cross-border financial planning. Not only does it affect taxation but it also may—depending on specific country rules—determine what, if any, marital property regime and/or forced heirship regime might affect your planning. Therefore, one of the first steps in analysis will be to determine the effect of citizenship or nationality in each of the jurisdictions in which you and your family members live, own assets, or receive income.

In the United States, the term "national" usually means someone who has U.S. nationality but not U.S. citizenship. The right to vote is the only major difference in this situation. Although at one time the United States was unique in applying its wealth transfer taxes on a worldwide basis to its citizens, the Philippines and Japan now apply wealth transfer taxes to their citizens whether domiciled in that country or overseas.

People who were born outside of the United States, who do not live and/or have never lived in the United States and who own no assets deemed to be located in the United States, but who have U.S. citizenship, are fully subject to the U.S. estate and gift tax regime. Because most countries throughout the world tax worldwide only if the taxpayer is "domiciled" or "resident" in that country (with a variety of definitions) the U.S. reach based solely on citizenship comes as a great surprise to many dual citizens born outside of the United States.

Another caveat that affects internationally mobile people is the whole subject of dual nationality. It should first be pointed out that some countries do not permit dual nationality while others only allow a very limited form of dual citizenship. Put simply, dual citizenship or dual nationality is not something that you directly apply for, although some countries are now offering this. It's more a matter of not renouncing the citizenship of one country in favor of another (unless you are forced).

Domicile

In the estate tax and property transfer context, the applicable concept is ordinarily "domicile" rather than residence, connoting a longer-term relationship with the jurisdiction. This will be compared to merely a short-term physical presence (which might cause residency status to exist for income tax purposes). If such domicile exists, the country may exercise taxing rights on the assets (worldwide or in the given jurisdiction) of the person. In these circumstances properties identified as personal to the individual will be deemed to have their situs at the domicile location.

Internationally mobile people and those with families of dual citizenship must be cautious of how a given country defines the term domicile as they vary from country to country.

Domicile is a long-established concept rooted in English common law. Generally speaking, domicile refers to the country to which an individual belongs, the country which is his natural home in which he resides and intends to remain permanently or indefinitely, or if absent, the country to which he intends ultimately to return.

In the United Kingdom, for example, concepts of domicile of origin, domicile of dependency, and domicile of choice, apply. Recent changes have created the concept of deemed domicile, which pertains to non-UK domiciled individuals who have been resident in the United Kingdom for fifteen of the past twenty years.

As I already mentioned, the definition of domicile is often made up of two important components: physical presence and intention. Once these two requirements are met, then it no longer matters if the person remains in the given country. For example, the United States estate and gift tax will apply to transfers made by such a person deemed "domiciled" in the U.S., regardless of where they live (or die) and regardless of the fact that all of the assets may be located outside of the United States.

Interestingly, even an illegal immigrant who has no legal right to be in the United States but whose intent can be shown to be to "stay" in the United States can be (and has been) fully subject to the U.S. estate tax at death, on a worldwide basis.

It is also entirely possible that more than one country will claim someone as domiciled in that country, at the same time. Apart from the possibility of tax relief from tax treaties between certain countries, there is no international body that would limit the claim of domicile to only one country.

Some jurisdictions (e.g. Switzerland) regard a person taking up domicile with the jurisdiction as resident. Under the Swiss law, domicile means the place at which an individual resides with the intention of settling.

Domicile should be distinguished from nationality; however, in the situation where a country is divided into separate states or legal systems, different rules apply. In the common law, upon birth, every person acquires domicile. This is the relationship between a person and a specific legal system. Subsequently, one might have an Australian nationality and a domicile in New South Wales, or an American nationality and a domicile in Texas. Although a person can, in some situations have dual nationality, it is not possible to have more than one domicile at a time. Two countries may claim domicile, but by definition it's not possible.

Residence

The domestic tax laws of most countries contain specific rules for determining whether an individual is resident within the country or jurisdiction for tax purposes. These rules are independent of immigration rules. Therefore, a person resident under the immigration law of the jurisdiction may or may not be a resident under the domestic tax law and vice versa.

The determination of residence often rests on a "facts and circumstances" test, which looks at the various social and economic connections the person has to the taxing jurisdiction as well as the person's intent with regard to his stay and his connections to other jurisdictions. The facts and circumstances test renders an individual resident if a person has personal or economic ties (e.g., residence of family, nationality, permanent home, principal source of income, employment, etc.) with the jurisdiction. This general test is frequently supplemented with a mechanical test based on the number of days present in the jurisdiction. Residence for tax purposes may or may not be connected with residence in terms of immigration status.

The term "residence" has different meanings for immigration, income tax, charitable giving and wealth transfer purposes both across and within jurisdictions. Because of this, broad assumptions as to similarities among jurisdictions can lead to various traps.

Residency Shifting Can Lead to Unintended Dual Residency

Although aspects of tax law may treat a family as a single unit, this unified treatment may not apply to issues of residency and domicile. For planning purposes it's important to note that because each member of a family may be considered individually, there is some scope for intra-family planning. There can also be some trouble if this is not carried out correctly or if a family member doesn't pay attention to details.

For example, consider the following situation: Husband is a citizen of Country A. Husband marries Wife, who is a citizen of Country B. Initially they decide to live together in Country B. Husband retains assets in Country A, solely, despite living in Country B and files tax returns separate from Wife (who, remember is not a citizen or resident or owner of assets in Country A). Wife owns assets in Country B solely and pays taxes on income and assets in Country B. Their children are born in Country B. Several years later, for varying reasons, Husband takes employment back in Country A, while Wife and children work and go to school in Country B. Gradually, Wife and children spend more time visiting Husband. Wife obtains driver's license in Country A and a child begins school in Country A.

I hope you can see by this illustration that this family is looming closer and closer to Wife having a closer connection to Country A and residency may be triggered now or in the near future if the established pattern continues.

2. How are the countries relevant for purposes of our tax filter?

Once we know what countries or localities are relevant, we look at the different type of tax that can apply.

At the basic level, countries may tax:

1. Residents on foreign income.

   For example, a resident of Canada may own common stock of a company incorporated in India. The income from the shares in the Indian company (dividends) would be considered taxable by Canada. In this situation, a country is applying the "residence" principle of taxation.

2. Non-residents on income arising in the given country.

   For example, India would be able to tax the resident of Canada on the income from the stock, since the stock is from an Indian company. In this situation, the "source" principle of taxation is being applied.

   Additionally, many non-U.S. citizens purchase real estate and investment assets located in the United States. If the investment assets are held in a U.S. brokerage account, withholding, by the United States withholding agent, of tax on dividends, for example, will occur. The standard rate of withholding is 30%, although if you are resident outside of the U.S. in a tax-treaty country, it is possible that a lower rate of withholding on income will apply.

   Most countries and jurisdictions do not apply either the residence or the source principle solely or purely, but rather most tax systems use a mixture of the two.

   There are many types of tax beyond income tax. These taxes may include property taxes, social security taxes, general wealth tax, sales taxes and custom duties, to name a few.

   A wealth tax is based on a person's net worth. Currently a few countries asses a wealth tax on its residents, including Colombia,

Spain[13], Italy, France, and Norway. Switzerland assesses a wealth tax at the canton and municipality level, but not at the Federal level.

In addition, Zakat, an Islamic "wealth tax" is levied to Muslim citizens of Pakistan, Malaysia, Sudan and Yemen. Similarly, Zakat is payable by Saudis and citizens of Gulf Cooperation Council states, resident in Saudi Arabia.

Clearly, there is little uniformity among the tax systems of the countries of the world and given the varied connecting factors, such as residence and/or domicile, it is possible to have more than one jurisdiction seeking to tax the same income or asset. The creation of tax treaties between countries seeks to mitigate this problem. However, you should know that not all countries have treaties in place and in certain situations the treaties do not provide complete guidance.

Possible Exposure to Foreign Death Taxes

Families with assets located in more than one country often have questions about the transfer taxes that may be imposed at the time of death by the foreign jurisdiction(s) where those assets are located.

In addition, families who have family members living permanently in different countries will be interested in having this same information. Thus, as in the example above, in which a person holds a portfolio of U.S. and foreign securities, it will be important to determine which assets the United States will consider located in its jurisdiction for estate and gift tax purposes. It will also be important to determine how the home or domicile country will treat these assets.

---

[13] Net wealth tax was abolished in Spain, but the Spanish government reinstated the tax initially for years 2011 and 2012, and then extended it to 201, 2014, 2015, 2016 and 2017. It is expected to be extended in future years.

The following section introduces some of the different wealth transfer taxes that can apply in a cross-border context.

Types of Foreign Country Transfer Taxation

A wide variety of taxation techniques might be encountered in foreign countries when transfers of family wealth are made, including the following:

1. *Transfer taxation.* This tax is based on the specific event of a property transfer.

2. *Inheritance taxation.* This is a more common tax outside of common law countries. The inheritance tax is imposed on the recipient of the transferred wealth when received. This tax is not imposed on the transfer of wealth but, rather, on the increase of wealth occurring to the beneficiary of a property transfer. The inheritance tax rate applicable to such transfers may vary, depending on the degree of relationship between the transferor and the recipient of the property transferred. A lower tax rate may be applicable if the recipient is a spouse or a minor child of the transferor, with the highest rate being applicable when the recipient is a quite remote relative or is unrelated.

3. *Inclusion* of the transferred property in the income of the recipient. The taxation of a transfer of wealth is dealt with under the applicable income tax system, rather than under a separate wealth transfer taxation system. The receipt of the gratuitous transfer is treated as an accession to wealth of the transferee for purposes of measuring income for a particular tax year.

4. *Capital Gains Tax.* This tax is imposed at the time of death, or as of an earlier transfer. Under this system, the gains accumulated up to the date of death (or the time of an earlier transfer) are recognized on the transfer of the property. The deemed transfer at death is treated as a property disposition event. The gain

amount is included in the income tax base in the local country. This gain is sometimes taxed at a preferential tax rate.

These are merely examples of the varying family property transfer taxation techniques that may be applicable in certain countries. The precise rules in the relevant country need to be carefully investigated with the assistance of local counsel.

Trap: In some jurisdictions, it is the "domicile" of the beneficiary that is relevant. In other jurisdictions, it is the "domicile" of the person transferring the property at death that is critical and it is irrelevant where the beneficiary lives.

Conflicting Claims of Tax Jurisdiction

Double taxation arises due to the overlap of fiscal sovereignty at the domestic level or international level. For example, multiple powers may exist within a country between federal and state governments. Internationally, two tax jurisdictions may claim the tax residency of a person.

As a result, the overlapping exercise of tax jurisdiction can lead to three types of conflicting claims that we need to be aware of in our cross-border financial planning:

1. Two or more countries claim that the same income of a taxpayer is sourced in their countries under their tax laws.

2. Two or more countries regard the same taxpayer as a tax resident in their countries ('dual residence').

3. The same income is taxed twice, both by the source country, where the income is taxable under its source of income rules and in the country in which the taxpayer is resident under the residence rules.

Many of these tax issues arise due to lack of consistency in tax rules and practices in different countries. Each country follows its own tax practices and applies the interpretation under its own legal system. Some of the common reasons for tax conflicts include:

1. Varying definitions of tax terms, and classification of transactions (revenue or capital) in different countries. For example, the meaning of terms which are commonly used in domestic law and treaties (such as income tax, total income, residence, domicile, immovable property, etc.) may vary considerably according to the context.

2. Differences in "connecting factors" and tax computation rules applied in different jurisdictions. For example, foreign credit calculations made under domestic tax rules to relieve double taxation may not coincide with the basis applied in the source country. More than one country may claim an income or gain as arising from within its jurisdiction.

3. The legal nature of the taxpayer (e.g., individual, company, trust, partnership, etc.) may affect the tax rate and the tax computations. Different jurisdictions may characterize them differently under their domestic law.

In this aspect of the planning process, your advisory team is likely to spend a good deal of time engaged in defensive tax planning.

Although the financial planner may not be qualified to provide advice concerning the aspects of financial and tax planning in another country, he or she should have as much knowledge concerning foreign tax systems as possible. This knowledge enables the advisor to deal more effectively with specialist advisors in the given country and to be in a position to suggest alternative methods for structuring transactions that provide for the achievement of your goals under the laws of the countries involved, as much as possible.

This intersection of domestic tax law and the tax law of a foreign country is one of the most challenging features of financial planning in a cross-border context. At this point you are possibly more knowledgeable about how this all works, even if you don't have all the details, then many financial planners out there.

When you have two countries where you have a connection and they are both interested in the same income or transfer, the final question to ask is: Can a tax treaty help?

Income, Estate and Gift Tax Treaties

One avenue for relief from the taxation of income or an estate in more than one country is to determine whether or not there is a tax treaty between each of the countries involved.

If you are a resident of a country that has entered into a tax treaty with the United States or have received income from one of those countries, you may be able to claim benefits allowed by the treaty to lower the overall tax due. The treaty will determine which country has the right to tax and at what rates. In situations where an individual is determined to have residency in two countries, tiebreaker rules apply.

For the most up-to-date information and listing of countries that have income tax treaties with the United States, see:
https://www.irs.gov/businesses/international-businesses/united-states-income-tax-treaties-a-to-z.

Similarly, for a list of countries that have estate and gift tax treaties with the United States, visit:
https://www.irs.gov/businesses/small-businesses-self-employed/estate-gift-tax-treaties-international

In Section Three, you will see tax treaties referenced so you will want to make note to yourself that if you want to look up the treaties the links are located here.

I realize the last chapter was probably a lot for you to get through, but seriously, just keep the high level concepts in your head; that is what is really is important here. This is where I see a lot of confusion and where mistakes are made. By remembering these concepts you can save a lot of headaches, stress and money.

In keeping with our movement through the pillars of *Life + Wealth Achievement Formula,* now that you have an understanding of the concepts behind how "you at work" (i.e., income from using your Human Capital) and "your capital at work" (i.e., income produced by your Financial Capital), can be taxed and why, we can move on to one of those areas of great interest to most people: Cash Design.

7

CASH DESIGN

Let's take a moment to recap what you've accomplished so far.

We started by talking about the idea that clarity equals power. Clarity for your life comes from knowing *what* you want and why you want it.

You've taken a money inventory and a life inventory.

The money inventory provides you with a baseline for how you expect to allocate the money you generate during the planning period from human capital or financial capital, or some combination.

The life inventory helps you discover and then choose what you want to have, be or do in the eight focus areas of your life and why these are important to you. We addressed the fact that "the how" can be tedious, frustrating and a lot of work, so if you don't have a compelling enough reason "why" you're not likely to persevere through "the how."

I expanded your thinking from focusing only on the ideal outcome for each of the eight areas of life to include thinking about your minimally acceptable outcomes. This creates a range of view. This range of options is critical to keep your planning moving forward and not stalling out.

You filtered your ideal and minimally acceptable goals into your top ten for this year while carrying out a balance check to be sure you're giving appropriate, maybe equal, attention to all the areas of focus you chose for this year. You might have found that you needed to shift a goal to the minimally acceptable version so that you can devote more time or resources to another goal to allow for some more balance in your life.

Finally, you chose up to three of your top ten goals for your list of non-negotiable goals.

Coming into this step, if you involved your partner, you have a lot to work with, which is way more than most people have. You have what you need to now move into strategy building.

Before I walk you through the strategy-setting process, I want to address the planning tool that we are creating in this section: the spending plan.

Tell Your Money How to Support Your Life

When any couple, mobile or not, sits down to review finances, there is often tension. This tension is aggravated in cross-border situations by the costs associated with moving into a new home. If the decisions are left to be made in the first few days that you have arrived in your new home, then often decisions about buying everything from a car and new appliances down to shampoo can be made in the same breath and on the same day. In these situations, money disappears, often depleting bank accounts in a matter of hours.

A spending plan is different from the traditional budget that most of us are familiar with. Ideally, the spending plan reflects the short-term, intermediate and long-term goals that you have set for yourself and your family. The Life +Wealth Compass is one of the tools that can assist in goal setting. At a minimum, the spending plan represents your conscious decisions about your spending over the coming twelve months. The spending plan allows you to think about various categories of daily living and enter numbers that represent the outflow in the column that corresponds to its frequency. If used prior to the actual relocation, the spending plan can assist in providing a smoother transition. The spending plan is a vital tool for the two-career, two-income family that sees one spouse transferred overseas and the other spouse unable to work at all or for a period of time. In this situation, scenarios can be built showing the situation assuming the spouse does not work at all, among other scenarios.

If you are planning to maintain a residence in more than one country, you'll need to include the costs associated with each residence in your annual spending plan. In certain client situations, we have created a spending plan for each residence to capture the approximated lifestyle expenses, taxes, etc. associated with the country and residence. For overall planning purposes, these spending plans are then summarized on a Statement of Cash Flow. For most, getting the planned expenses in writing is an important first step toward a rich and rewarding cross-border life.

The spending plan and its accompanying cash management plan, can be a standing agenda item for your family meeting. Financial arguments usually are over how money will be spent and who's going to control the purse strings. While talking about money and how it can be used to support the needs of the individual members of the family creates tension, this tension tends to disappear over time as you and your family get used to talking about these issues. Avoiding them altogether only leads to disaster.

A spending plan is not another name for a budget. Money gurus have been preaching to create a budget and live within its confines for the last several decades. On the surface, this might be good advice, but in my experience there are a few major challenges with a budget and the act of budgeting if you want to create a financial strategy that is moving you sequentially closer to a life of your design.

First, most goal setting and budgeting conversations start by focusing on your income. Why is this? On the one hand this could be a natural thought, because it's logical that you can only spend what you actually receive. On the other hand, it could be because many aspects of personal finance were adopted from the corporate world. Specifically, departmental budgets are created as a result of the amount of "income" they are allocated. Here's the challenge: if you focus first on income, you condition your brain to disconnect from what the income is supposed to cover. It's my experience that the goals of people who focus on the income side of planning first are non-specific. For example, a goal might be to increase business revenue by 25% or a personal goal is to find a new job that has a "better" total compensation package. If asked to define "better" or generally for more specifics, another non-specific comment such as "I want to make more money so I can have a better lifestyle" follows. This approach tricks us. We make up a number that sounds good and then we attempt to commit to it. If you focus on income first, you don't know what you are trying to achieve; therefore, there is no context and no emotional connection. Only by knowing the cost of your desired life can you articulate a target income grounded in reality.

Second, the expense side of a budget is focused on past expenditures. All budget creation instructions that focus this way first require us to comb through receipts to figure out where the money went and use that information to determine how to spend this year. When I was a newly licensed financial planner, I followed this line of thinking because it's taught in most textbooks. I dutifully asked people to fill out our financial data forms based on their past expenditures. As you can imagine, this request was not popular and most of the time, we ended up combing through bank statements and receipts for the client so that I could move the process forward and get to the work I was actually being paid to do. Most people don't like the accounting function and they are looking for more time for themselves and their family, not another thing to do with their time. So, usually this just doesn't get done.

But, let's say you're an exception. You like accounting so you make the time to do this. I assume you are using this strategy to make this year your best year ever because you want to make changes to improve your overall satisfaction in life and in your finances. So, let me ask you a question. If you keep repeating the past, how can you possibly achieve what you want this year? You can't achieve something new by doing the same thing as before. Budgets are focused on past expenditures as a guide to the future. They assume not much will change. If you don't plan on having more money than you had last year or being more financially focused this year than you were last year, or having a year where your money better supports your life, then budgeting could work for you. If not, a budget or the act of traditional budgeting will actually limit your progress.

The traditional approach that we are taught to use — to look at the expenditure from past years isn't strategic. It doesn't tie into your top goals for this year. It doesn't balance the concepts of money past, money present, and money future.

Many gurus seem to advocate budgeting as a disguise for a way for us to save more. They ask you to see how you could save an extra $100 or so by cutting out things like daily cappuccinos. In this respect, budgeting is almost like a diet that was prescribed for you.

I don't believe that traditional budgeting is a particularly effective tool for people. The truth is budgeting started as a tool to manage government. It was later adopted by companies and was most recently adopted for individuals as personal financial planning came into existence.

Although money management has been around as long as money has existed, the idea of a budget is a recent concept, often attributed to the British monarchy in the 1700s. At that time, budgeting was mainly self-serving since the first controls were put on the military so the king couldn't create a force to overthrow Parliament. However, things were rarely written down, there wasn't a regular review and no reporting took place.

By the early 18th century, officials of the king delivered his plans on how to spend the money that Parliament would allocate. The term "budget" actually came from the Latin word for the bag in which these plans were carried. It later came to mean the plans themselves.

We can't talk about budgets and not talk about the related concept of category percentages and those general rules of thumb.

Financial Ratios and Rules of Thumb

Many books and some programs provide guidelines or so-called "rules of thumb" for how much of our spending should be allocated on a percentage basis to various groups of expenses. These vary but some general examples are ten or so percent allocated to savings and investment, no more than thirty percent of income for a monthly mortgage payment, no more than five percent of your expenses should be allocated to so-called "luxury items" — you get what I'm talking about here.

Financial rules of thumb are widely discussed and contentiously debated among financial professionals and academics. I think this is often due to a combination of competing interests but it's also most likely due to different assumptions made to arrive at the suggested percentage allocation. That said this phenomenon is not uncommon when a number of variables exist in wholly different situations and stages of life, which can render even the best approach to expense or income allocation guidelines ineffective.

No ratios or rules can encompass the intricacies of multiple variables, life stages, market factors and geographic locations. With the sheer number of guidelines that exist, much like diets, it is understandable that we become frustrated and overwhelmed in the process and then conclude that money management is both confusing and hard.

The point is, these rules of thumb are based on a life path (in the form of a set of assumptions) that has been predetermined for you. The author or creator of the program is giving you guidelines because first of all, they aren't teaching you how to think or how to know what is the right allocation for you. They're giving you a shortcut because they assume you either can't or won't do the work.

Whoever designed the rule of thumb effectively created a strategy for you to follow. They did the thinking for you and wrote you a prescription of sorts. Usually that is why these programs are not sustainable. This reminds me of the proverb that says, "Give a man a fish and you feed him for a day. Teach a man to fish and you feed him for a lifetime." Instead of teaching you how to fish, they are giving you fish. In this section of the book, we're focused on how to create your own strategy, and specifically we're focused on building strategy to cover both twelve months of living expenses and your goals for this year. Please understand that there is no right or wrong allocation, only decisions. If you make decisions using this process, based on the context of your "what and why" your decisions will usually move you closer to increased life satisfaction together with financial stability or financial freedom.

As we move into building strategy and you start to see percentages I want you to use them as the analytical tools they are. Use the ratios as benchmarks. Don't get caught up initially on what is an appropriate percentage. Evaluate it in the context of how your life feels along with common sense. For example, if your commitment bucket figure is sixty percent of total annual expenses but you're still paying a mortgage and have a couple of kids in private school or college and you are funding all of these through current income, then maybe that's a reasonable number. Contrast it with someone who is childless, has a mortgage but has large revolving credit card debt and whose commitment bucket is also sixty percent of total expenditures. I'm sure that while there is probably some stress in both situations, each of those people knows where the stress is coming from and what they can or cannot change. Over time you'll be able to determine your own percentages based on your life path, and as I mentioned earlier, as circumstances change so do category percentages. All plans need flexibility. Rules of thumb cannot provide flexibility because they are based on a single set of assumptions that may or may not align with your own.

Let's now move on to spending plans by first understanding what a spending plan is not. A spending plan—the way that we are creating one—is not simply another name for a budget. There are advisors who believe that a spending plan is a different name for a budget but that is because they accept the traditional concept of a budget. We are taking a different approach altogether.

What is a Spending Plan?

Your spending plan is the written document that will carry out your financial plan for the year. It assumes that you undertook strategic thinking to produce it. It isn't just a carry forward from a previous year. Your spending plan is usually visualized through a household-spending plan and one or more individual spending plans.

Taken together the spending plans provide a guide for how your money will move through various bank and/or financial accounts. Your spending plans are a way to map out your strategy on paper before you set up or amend any deposit or transfer standing orders with your financial institutions.

At the simplest level, all income and expenses flow through a single household-spending plan. In this situation all income and expenses are flowing into a joint account for couples and a single primary account for an individual. Your household account should be seen as your primary working account. In nearly all other situations, individual spending plans are created in conjunction with a household-spending plan.

Some couples decide to have two individual accounts in addition to a jointly owned, household account for each to use as she or he wishes. This allows each partner to feel empowered and in control of their money, while at the same time working together to manage the household funds. In this situation, financial privacy is valued by the partners and exercised through the use of both "our" money and "my" money.

When there is more than one country or currency involved, there may be more than one set of spending plans linking together with the base currency spending plans.

Let's now shift into the strategy building so that you will have the spending plans we just introduced. As we move through this material, you may want to refer to the worksheet that you can find in the book resources vault.

Spending Plan Strategy Setting Process

To build your strategy you're going to need the Money Inventory Worksheet and the work from your Life Inventory.

Step 1. Transfer the Bucket totals from the Money Inventory Worksheets to the Spending Plan Strategy Builder Worksheet.

Remember that we are working in monthly totals.

Spending Plan Strategy Building Worksheet

Commitment Bucket Total
(transfer from the Commitment Bucket page)

Commitment Bucket Surplus/Deficit
(Source 1 Income - Commitment Bucket total)

Consumption Bucket Total
(Add all sub-totals together)

Consumption Bucket Surplus/Deficit
(Source 1 Income - Consumption Bucket total)

Coming Bucket Total
(transfer from the Coming Bucket total above)

Coming Bucket Surplus/Deficit
(Source 1 Income - Coming Bucket total)

Total Monthly Spending
(Add the Bucket totals above)

Projected Income (Source 1)

Commitment Bucket Surplus/Deficit
(Source 2 Income - Commitment Bucket total)

Surplus/(deficit)

Projected Income (Source 2)

Consumption Bucket Surplus/Deficit
(Source 2 Income - Consumption Bucket total)

Surplus/(deficit)

Projected Income (Source 3)

Coming Bucket Surplus/Deficit
(Source 2 Income - Coming Bucket total)

Surplus/(deficit)

Total Projected Monthly Income

Step 2. Determine Baseline Monthly Spending

Add the totals you transferred over to obtain your baseline monthly spending amount. If you are a sole proprietor or business owner, total spending is the baseline figure for minimum profit your business needs to produce for this period.

Your total annual spending total can be looked at in two ways:

One. It's the cost of living your life this year.

Two. It's the amount of money you will have to make this year. Your total spending number represents how much money you must earn to fund your life for the year. The simple fact of knowing this number, believe it or not, can ease loads of financial pressure. Your number enables you to know how much money is enough for the year. If you know you need to earn more, now you know how much. This removes the guesswork. If you have little control over your income number then you'll need to make sure your cost of living your life does not exceed your income. If you do have control over your income, then this is the number used to set your business, career or investment income goals.

Step 3. Allocate Income

First, think about your expected sources of income. You may have more than one. For example, you may have net take home income from employment, investment income or income from a business. Label them source 1, source 2, etc.

Source 1 is typically the primary and most stable source of income for yourself or your family.

We enter that in the projected income box and then subtract total monthly spending from income source one and we enter that number in the surplus or deficit row.

Then we add in the other expected income, repeating the process until all income has been allocated.

Step 4. Determine Positioning For New Goal Funding

Subtracting Total Monthly Spending from Total Monthly Income from income source 1 gives you the net surplus or shortfall. This provides some immediate insight and perspective.

How well positioned are you? The amounts you calculate here will leave you concluding one of three things:

1. You earn enough income to cover the baseline living expenses per your Money Inventory, and there is surplus that can still be allocated for goals.

2. You earn enough income to cover the baseline living expenses per your Money Inventory, but there is not sufficient surplus to allocate to goals.

3. You don't earn enough to cover the baseline living expenses per your Money Inventory.

If you are in situation 1, move on to the next step in the process.

If you are in situation 2, decide if you can and want to adjust your baseline Money Inventory so that you can include the costs of one or more of your non-negotiable items. Adjust to the point that you have surplus that covers the goal(s) and then move on to the next step. Be sure to adjust the who-and-how-much section for any changes you make.

If you are in situation 3:

1. Make a copy of the baseline Money Inventory and label this Option 1.

2. Referring to the Spending Plan Strategy Building Worksheet, look closer at the surplus or deficit following allocation of income to your Commitment Bucket. Answer the question: How much of your consumption bucket and Coming Bucket cannot be funded at this point?

3. Using the Money Inventory labeled Option 1, make adjustments to the Consumption Bucket that allow you to keep the allocations to the Coming Bucket or adjust the Coming Bucket to allow you to keep the allocations to the Consumption Bucket. The goals that you want for this year may need to be pushed to the following year unless the cost can replace something else in the same category. Choose whether to stop here or adjust (create option 2, etc.) until you have sufficient surplus that covers the goal(s) and then move on to the next step.

4. Make sure the *who-and-how-much* sections have been updated for any changes.

Step 5. Fund Non-negotiables

Create a copy of the baseline money inventory. Starting with the costs of the non-negotiable goals you set, add the costs associated with the non-negotiables until you have zero surplus or a minimal amount of surplus. Adjust consumption costs if needed. If you still have surplus move to step 6, otherwise stop here.

Step 6. Fund remaining goals

Adjust the non-negotiables version of the money inventory until you are satisfied that you have funded the most important goals. Be sure to adjust the *who-and-how-much* sections of the money inventory as well.

Step 7. Transfer your totals to the spending plan worksheets for each of your household account and individual accounts.

"Individual Account"	Currency : USD		"Household Account"	Currency : USD
CASH INFLOWS	Monthly		CASH INFLOWS	Monthly
Net Earned Income	4,725.00		Income Contribution to Household Ac - Indiv 1	10,100.00
Bonus	0		Income Contribution to Household Ac - Indiv 2	3,000.00
Other Income	0		Other Income	0
Total Cash Inflows	4,725.00		Total Cash Inflows	13,100.00
CASH OUTFLOWS	Monthly		CASH OUTFLOWS	Monthly
Commitment Bucket			Commitment Bucket	
Contribution to Household Plan/Account	3,000.00		Rent	0
Contribution to Other Currency Plan/Account	500.00		First Mortgage	0
Rent				

"Individual Account"	Currency : USD		"Household Account - Currency 2"	Currency : CAD
CASH INFLOWS	Monthly		CASH INFLOWS	Monthly
Net Earned Income	11,180.50		Income Contribution to Household Ac - Indiv 1	0
Cost of Living Adjustment	2,837.00		Income Contribution to Household Ac - Indiv 2	611.54
Other Income HOUSING ALLOWANCE	7,083.33		Other Income	0
Total Cash Inflows	21,100.83		Total Cash Inflows	611.54
CASH OUTFLOWS	Monthly		CASH OUTFLOWS	Monthly
Commitment Bucket			Commitment Bucket	
Contribution to Household Plan/Account	10,100.00		Rent	0
Contribution to Other Currency Plan/Account	0		First Mortgage	0
Rent	7,000.00			

Congratulations! You have an agreed upon cash flow plan. You may notice that you need to allocate transfers between accounts to carry out the plan you just created.

A couple of notes here: First, only allocate investment income as a source if you plan to spend it this year. And only enter sources of income you actually need to support the total expenses.

Second, if you have a situation where you have a startup business as well as regular recurring income, I suggest you set the income target from the startup using the amount not funded once goals are added in, but for spending plan purposes you use the figures from baseline work.

If your situation involves a young business with irregular income, then only allocate, as an income source, what you *absolutely know* you can take home each month in the form of net annual profit or net monthly wages. Your business income and expenses must be completely separate from your personal accounts. Allocate any extra income to retained earnings and then at the end of the year consider how much you can increase your base wages in the coming year when you repeat this process. Be sure to factor in expense reimbursement as well.

How to Handle Planning For an Irregular Income

An irregular income can make it difficult to plan and succeed financially. When you're not sure how much money you'll have from month to month, it can be difficult to plan. Let's talk some more about the tips and tricks you can do now so you'll have a steady amount to plan for each month. The goal here is to plan to reduce the probability of an income crisis.

Tip One: Work a month out. One of the best things you can do is to live on the bare minimum that you know you can easily bring in each month. If you can't, then you need to set up your spending strategy to live on basic income each month and save any excess monthly income to cover those additional things you want to spend money on this year. To make this work, you'll want to work off the previous month's income. This allows you to know exactly how much money you will have to spend for the next month. If you're working a job where you are paid on commission each week, or if you're working for tips it can be easy to dip into those funds to cover your bills right now. If you set aside extra each week until you reach the amount of your very basic living needs, it will help you to normalize your spending plan and make it easier to pay your bills each month. Once you've done this, you can contribute the money into a savings account each week, until you have enough saved up to pay yourself the next month. The extra money you earn after that can go to other expenses.

Tip Two: Save for lean months. In addition to saving up so you can live on last month's wages, you need to save up for the lean months. This means you should have a financial account to cover the months where you do not make enough to get by. Every month you earn enough to cover the next month's expenses, you should be putting money into a savings account to cover a month where your sales drop or to cover yourself if you cannot work as much as you normally do. If your salary is completely commission based, you may want more than one month's income in the fund, and if you have a base pay, you may want to save the difference between your base pay and your basic spending for a few months. This is different from a traditional emergency fund. If you are building a business that is not run as a sole proprietorship then set up another business account for this purpose so you get a better sense of cash flow peculiarities that are unique to your business.

Tip Three: Finalize your Money Inventory worksheets so that you have a zero balance — no surplus or deficit remaining after you allocate all your planned income sources, and come up with a final version. As you do that, start thinking about those expenses in terms of *who and how much.*

The first time through this will be hard, without question. It's a new process to you. Also going into the next round, you'll have familiarity so it will be easier. The more often you do something, the more skilled you'll become at it.

Having controlled cash flow, we can now move into financial capital.

8

FINANCIAL CAPITAL

How to approach planning for and funding longer-term goals and aspirations.

When an investment policy takes account of a family's various goals, its likely future inflows and outflows, currency requirements, and available investment alternatives, the family feels an increased level of security and satisfaction, because there is a strategic plan in place to assure that it has the resources to achieve its goals across the personal, financial, and social dimensions of wealth.

All too often, clients approach investment planning as though it is separate from the rest of their financial lives by making tactical, short-term decisions on money that will be used to fund long-term objectives. Many internationally-mobile people, use this approach because their future plans are uncertain. They may move again to another country, or don't know where they want to retire. Perhaps they can't agree on or aren't sure where the kids will go to university, or they have a hard time sifting through the myriad investment options available to them. Because there is no strategic plan in place, the investments, which are strategic tools, are being subject to the same daily living decisions, when they need to have a strategic direction. That is not to suggest that your investment policy does not take short-term goals and planning issues into consideration, as it absolutely should. However, your investment policy is only as good as the planning analysis that supports it.

The field of investment is vast, particularly at the global level. Therefore, as with the previous chapters on the technical planning issues, I won't attempt to cover it all. The point of this chapter is to highlight some of the key investment issues that deserve special attention in the context of a cross-border or multinational financial planning situation. Above all, all cross-border families—from individuals and couples on international assignment to multinational families and everyone in situations in between—should ensure that their investment planning is consistent with and matched to their various objectives.

This chapter outlines a more comprehensive view of investment policy than many internationally mobile people and transnational families adopt. I cover more than just investment issues, including day-to-day cash management, long-term projections of sources and uses of cash, development and application of risk models, development of a target asset allocation and systematic portfolio rebalancing and review.

This set of tasks is outside the normal scope of most investment managers who are not trained in the area of investment management consulting or financial planning and the necessary modeling of various scenarios to arrive at a comprehensive and integrated financial plan that is supported by the investment policy.

Asset Allocation versus Investment Policy

Most investing literature available today stresses the importance of a concept known as *asset allocation*. Anyone whose employer sponsors a defined contribution pension plan should be somewhat familiar with this terminology. At the time you joined the plan and perhaps at least once a year since then, you've probably been asked to choose from a group of investment choices to determine what percentage of your pension plan is to be allocated to each. Having made your choices based on whatever information is provided to you, the end result is, by default, your "chosen" asset allocation. How does this occur? It's simple, really. Each investment option on the list provided can be boiled down from the broad asset class level (e.g., cash and equivalents, equity, fixed income, real estate, venture capital) to the geographic level (e.g., country-specific, regional, international) to market capitalization (e.g., small, mid, large) and to style (e.g., growth, value, sector, etc.) to determine its own asset allocation.

If you invest all of your pension funds into one option (perhaps the cash and equivalents option), then your overall asset allocation is clear, but when you invest in more than one option (which is necessary to provide for adequate diversification to offset risks), you can see how it is easy to lose track of exactly *how* your money is invested.

I have included this example to illustrate the point that blindly allocating your money to investments without first establishing an investment policy is like heading out on a road trip without a map. You'll probably get where you want to go, but it will take a lot longer and will be a lot more stressful.

The creation of an investment policy first requires a clear understanding of what the policy is to accomplish. What are the various goals that you want to achieve? When you work with your cross-border financial planner, he or she should be taking a comprehensive view toward your goals.

Throughout this section, I have provided information with regard to the specific areas that your financial planner will address. The way strategy is developed is through financial modeling. Components of the modeling process are also the guiding principles found in the investment policy. After all, the investment policy is what will put the plan into action. Most importantly, it is the tool you will use to measure the appropriateness of your investment decisions. The appropriateness will not be measured by rate of return alone but also by the *alignment* with the assumptions set out by the plan, illustrated by the *achievement* of your most important goals.

An Introduction to Cross-Border Life + Wealth Investing™

Individuals and families usually have multiple goals that take place over different time periods and each of these goals has different potential for being realized.

Life + Wealth Investing measures success by focusing on the achievement of specific life goals. *Cross-Border Life + Wealth Investing* goes one step further than *Life + Wealth Investing* by focusing on the achievement of life goals that are funded by more than one currency to support family, causes or assets in more than one country.

How different is it from "traditional" investing and why is this important?

The idea of setting goals for your investments may not seem particularly different or new. You've probably heard the topic of goals and objectives discussed by financial advisors before now. However, *Life + Wealth Investing* goes well beyond what you have seen or heard. *Life + Wealth Investing* and *Cross-Border Life + Wealth Investing* provide a more relevant way to measure investment performance than the traditional benchmarks.

Typically, your investments are put into a single, diversified portfolio, with allocation to different asset classes such as equity and fixed income based primarily on a measurement of volatility that you agree to as determined by your risk profile. For example, your portfolio may be characterized as "growth" or "balanced" (meaning that both fixed income and equity asset classes are included).

The traditional financial professional is effectively hired and held accountable for delivering a specific risk-return profile. Any withdrawals needed to meet your cash flow needs (aka goals) are typically met through the sale of a percentage of each investment to maintain the asset allocation percentages as dictated by the profile.

The question now becomes, how are we measuring success? If, for example, we focus on only the relative performance of the portfolio compared to an appropriate benchmark, we might decide that the portfolio is successful. However, if we measure success by the ability of the portfolio to deliver with a high degree of certainty the cash withdrawals required at the time needed over the entire time period the portfolio was designed to meet, we'll need more information to determine the success of the portfolio.

CROSS-BORDER LIFE + WEALTH INVESTING™ INVESTMENT POLICY FORMULATION SUMMARY

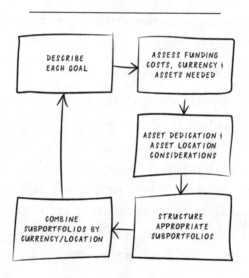

Careful asset allocation across different accounts such as a taxable brokerage, 401k, IRA, Roth IRA and a foreign pension is essential to achieve tax efficiency and maximum after-tax returns for successful retirement saving and greater overall wealth accumulation.

The investment plan should address the following:

- Anticipated contributions.

- Anticipated time frame for the various objectives the policy is to achieve.

- Anticipated taxation of the various assets.

- The expected dates and amounts for planned withdrawals.

- Impact of expenses to the achievement of the goals.

- Sequence of return risk and "time value of return fluctuation" and each of their impact (positive or negative) to the value of the portfolio, from which future distributions will be made over time.

- In other words, success is tied to the degree to which the portfolio survives or is not depleted.

- Uncertainty about the goals themselves?

The future is, by definition, unknown. Financial planning helps you make an informed decision based on analysis of the present structures, goals and other "known" factors, and the use of a model that quantifies the risks as much as possible, as well as possible outcomes. By simulating various scenarios, it is possible for you to evaluate the spectrum of trade-offs that are likely to occur. As a result, you are able to reduce the Paradox of Choice of decision-making that often hinders your move along the *Life + Wealth Map*.

An appropriate investment policy is a crucial component of your family's long-term approach to the philosophies you have drafted to guide the personal, financial and social dimensions of your life and wealth. Over time, this policy can also be critical to the achievement of you and your family's core values as carried out in your mission statement.

It's crucial because it relies on the central premise that you have taken the time to reflect on what is and is not working, right now, in your life and that of your family. It assumes that you have followed the steps to visualize your ideal for each of the *8 Facets of Daily Living,* that you have identified your core values and philosophies to guide your goals setting within the personal, financial and social dimensions of your life and wealth and that you have taken time to work with a cross-border financial planning team to identify some of the technical issues that must be addressed either prior to or during the modeling process. It's also crucial, because it assumed that all of this has been accomplished *before* you put the investment policy into place.

9

PROTECT THE PLAN

Reduce the Risk of Plan Failure

Once you've put the work into creating the plan that you are confident and excited about, it's time to focus on the risks that can cause that plan to fail.

There are many risks in everyday life that could have devastating effects on your assets, your family and your dreams. Unfortunate events like the death of a spouse, an automobile accident, sudden illness, disability of the primary income-earner and in certain areas, the risk of kidnap and ransom are a few examples. These risk exposures must be reviewed with every border crossing, and if permanently established, they should be revised periodically to ensure current risk management strategies are appropriate and new strategies selected as required.

The potential for exposure to new or additional risk exists with every new posting and every border crossing by the primary income-earner and family members. Consider the issues below as examples of potential risks. As with all areas of cross-border planning, be sure to give yourself enough time to carry out necessary analysis *before* crossing a border.

Personal Property Coverage

Insurance coverage applicable to an overseas move is very different from your typical domestic homeowners or tenants policy. Package policies, specifically designed to cover the unique aspects of international assignments, should be sought out and reviewed for the "best fit" in the context of your objectives.

Areas of coverage to be considered include:

- Coverage for items left in commercial storage.

- Transportation coverage on items shipped by sea, air, and truck.

- Coverage at your overseas residence for fire, theft, and natural perils.

- Protection for effects while traveling temporarily within the United States or other countries.

In certain cases, you may wish to consider *all risks* coverage, which provides broader protection as well as replacement cost coverage, assuring a non-depreciated claims settlement.

Be sure to check into the thoroughness of insurance provided by the shipping and packing company. Some policies may be inadequate or overly expensive. And don't forget to ask about what happens in the event of a loss.

You should also complete a full inventory of assets and personal effects before you move, sorted by *transported abroad* and *left in storage* or another location. This will help on a number of planning levels. The most obvious short-term advantage is that it will be of tremendous help should you be in the position of having to file a claim in the event of a loss.

Domestic Policies

If you are transferred overseas and intend to maintain a residence in your home country, your current coverage may need to be adjusted. For example, if the home that was your primary residence will now be rented out to others while you're abroad, you may find that your current homeowner's policy must be cancelled and written under a new policy that provides for fire and liability coverage.

International Major Medical Insurance

If you're not covered under a group medical insurance program, individual policies can be purchased. These policies include worldwide medical protection and also can include evacuation services. If you're transitioning for employment-related reasons, be sure that there are no gaps in coverage between contracts.

Life Insurance

Another area often overlooked is that of protection from various risk exposures due to the death of the primary income-earner. I have often seen executives with large insurance policies — with the company named as the beneficiary. While this is fine for the company, the problem is when the executive thinks the policy is for his or her family.

A significant hurdle to using life insurance to protect the contingent asset of future income against death is the policy itself. This is another example of where the jurisdictional issues are a challenge to the idea globalization and global mobility. Specifically, U.S. citizens and residents can obtain a policy that insures their life while resident in the United States, but they will need a so-called "expat policy" to insure the same life while *not* resident in the United States.

Life insurance is much easier to deal with on an international scale than it once was; however, it's still a significant challenge. In the past it was only possible to buy life insurance in your home country if you maintained an active connection there such as holding a driver's license, or maintaining a bank account. However, because of advances in communication through the Internet, international life insurance is generally more accessible.

If you already have life insurance through a major provider such as MetLife, you may find you don't have to change a thing except to provide the company with an address change and arrange payments from your existing American bank account. You could already be covered no matter where you live — however, you'll need to check with your current provider to see what the limitations of your policy are. If you are already living outside the United States, obtaining a policy from a U.S. insurance company may be a challenge.

Coverage shortfalls are always present in one form or another. One policy that has everything you need, no matter where you are, for a significant amount of time, does not exist.

Some U.S. citizens and residents obtain foreign life insurance while living abroad and are surprised to learn about the premium excise tax and reporting. They are even more surprised to learn that, in most cases, the policy will not cover them once they leave the country where it was issued.

You must also determine the impact of currency on your goals. Although your existing life policy may cover you in your new jurisdiction, the currency it will pay the life benefit in, may no longer be adequate. You should review all your policies to ensure your coverage is adequate and are structured in a way that does not trigger tax issues in certain countries.

For individuals who live in a country where there is economic or political instability, the possibility to purchase, hold and possibly borrow against a life policy, denominated in a stable currency, may be attractive in terms of asset protection and investment appreciation. As with any life insurance policy the owner of the policy may be a partnership, a company or a trust, depending on the planning advice that may arise after reviewing the specific issues, needs and goals.

Kidnap and Ransom

As executives follow investment and new business into emerging economies, they and their families are increasingly vulnerable to the crimes of kidnap, ransom and extortion. Even in safer areas of the world, the chance of being extorted is possible, and certain precautions should be taken, including the consideration of insurance coverage. It's important to work with experienced underwriters in this unique area of business so that complete protection can be achieved.

Imagine your loved one has just been released from abduction. The private negotiator was successful; the consultants you hired for interpretation and public relations did their jobs; the ransom was paid. You can go home. But now the reality sets in. You've liquidated your assets for the ransom, which thankfully wasn't lost during the delivery. The debt you've accumulated from travel expenses, communications costs, security and other professional fees are enormous, and the future expense of physical, psychiatric and medical rehabilitation along with legal counsel will be an incredible financial burden. If you had purchased a kidnap and ransom insurance policy or your employer had one in place, these expenditures would be taken care of.

This type of coverage is of increasing interest to individuals and families, businesses and corporations, doctor groups, educational institutions, missionary groups, financial institutions, athletic teams, film productions, boating enterprises, and private plane charters. There is insurance designed to indemnify the ransoms and numerous expenses incurred should a kidnapping take place. Some plans can also fund, without limit, the service of a crisis response team, and employing specialists located around the world.

Specifically, a policy may cover and/or provide:

- If the reimbursable ransom is "lost" during delivery, the plan can replace the funds.

- If there is a personal accident, the plan can indemnify medical expenses or pay a death benefit.

- Income lost due to the time it takes to handle a situation like this, and lost income can be included coverage.

Childcare can be considered as a recoupable cost.

- A crisis response team and professional consultation.

- Medical expenses, including psychiatric expenses and expenses for rest and relaxation, and cosmetic or plastic surgery after release.

- Loss due to injury such as mutilation, loss of fingers, total disability as a result of a kidnapping, and extortion or detention.

- Time away from work after release.

- Travel expenses.

- A reward paid to informants leading to the arrest and conviction of responsible parties.

- If the worst does happen, funeral expenses can be recovered.

It's a balancing act. In most kidnappings, the kidnappers demand that neither the authorities nor anyone else be notified. Balancing the demands of the kidnappers with the desire and need to contact the authorities is tough enough; imagine having to also decide whether or not to contact your insurance company. If you don't, the company may try to deny the coverage. If you do, you may jeopardize the situation. As a result, there is a need for silence with some policies including coverage exclusions if the existence of coverage is declared, after all "advertising" that such a policy exists could just invite the very risks you seek to insure.

Issues for consideration then include a policy that requires only a reasonable effort to see that awareness of the coverage is restricted as much as possible. This provides the policyholder latitude to use reasonable discretion in determining where and when to disclose the fact that the coverage is in place.

Some policies may require that you notify the insurance company and law enforcement officials about a kidnapping only when it's safe and practicable to do so. Obviously, any insurance policy term that has the potential to further imperil a victim's life should be deemed unenforceable. Selecting and negotiating more favorable provisions for these circumstances is far better than going to court over enforceability.

These policies often limit or exclude coverage or sometimes raise deductibles in regions and countries where travel or other warnings are issued. If your company, or the company you work for, does business in one of those places, and a family member or your employee is kidnapped there, the insurance company may try to limit or void coverage altogether. With kidnapping incidents seemingly on the rise, insurers are likely to expand such endorsements and exclusions even as they look to sell more kidnap/ransom policies. For the policyholder who gets past all these complexities, kidnap/ransom insurance can provide valuable services and guidance in addition to the potential reimbursement for a paid ransom.

If you are subject to the potential risks this type of policy is covers, the only thing worse than owning such problematic protection may be *not* owning it. The best you can do as a prudent insurance buyer or employee is to assess your needs, select a policy that is favorable for the corporation or family's endeavors and understand the policy's provisions, or tailor a policy so that it does.

SECTION THREE

CROSS-BORDER LIFE + WEALTH TACTICS, TOOLS AND TRAPS

In this section you'll learn why and how each physical or virtual border may affect your *Cross-Border Life + Wealth Achievement Plan*. Once you know the issues and some of the traps, you'll be able to adjust your strategy and then shift your attention to determining if any tactical changes are required to the assets, products and/or services used to carry out your strategy.

As you may remember from Section One, I noted that it is my experience that most people focus on their financial matters episodically and in segments and that this seems to be related to the fact that financial services are still typically delivered the same way: non-collaboratively and separately. In this situation, actions taken in one area typically have an impact on another area and thus, absent the reconciliation and integration of all of these segments, the result is a disconnected set of ideas that typically conflict with one another. So, the potential for conflict across strategies, high advisory fees, overwhelm and decision paralysis is exacerbated in the cross-border context. Therefore, it's important to be clear about the distinctions between strategy and tactics, as well as between context and content.

Strategy versus Tactics and Context versus Content

The best way to understand strategy versus tactics and context versus content is to think of a drinking glass. You have a dilemma: what will you put in the glass? Asking this question and the answer you arrive at is the detail, the content and the tactic. In science, it's the dependent variable.

When you read content such as this book or blog posts or articles or take a course, you need context to make the information useful. It's the same with tactical decisions, any *specific actions*, buying or selling anything is a *tactic* that absolutely must be considered in the *context of the strategy*.

Once you understand context, you know why what you're reading is relevant and therefore important or perhaps is *not* relevant and therefore is simply information.

Content Filtering

I get asked all the time "what do you think of [insert tactic or product name du jour here]"? I usually respond by asking for clarification: "What's important about said tactic?" or "Why is this important? By doing this I'm trying to understand the context. I'm asking for more information about whatever the thing is so I can determine relevance. Ultimately, it's the context that's going to drive what happens to the vision you have identified.

A lot of the work covered in Chapter 5, Life Design, can help you create your content filter.

How to Read This Section

You may want to use that content filter through this section of the book. My suggested approach is to skim read this entire section, making note of the content that is most relevant to you and your situation right now. Then, circle back to the specific chapters and/or sections that you want to read more carefully.

I'll catch up with you again the Conclusion.

10

CROSS-BORDER LIFE + WEALTH MINDSET

Introduction

If you want to change your life you have to change your strategy, you have to understand your story, and then decide what part of your story you want to keep and what needs to change.

If you're reading this book, you're in search of answers and strategies, to take control of your life, your money and your wealth, across country borders. You know that having the right strategy can save you time. If you start with a proven plan, the right strategy, you can literally convert decades of struggle into days of achievement. You can avoid the inevitable frustration that comes with learning something by trial and error.

But after years of creating strategy with and for clients, I know that strategy alone isn't enough. Sometimes our limiting stories keep us from finding the right strategies, or, if we have the right strategy, from executing it. Do you know anyone like that? You put the answer right in front of them and they still say "No, that will never work because..." They tell you a million reasons why it won't work — they have every excuse there is. If they have the right strategies, why aren't people using them? Why are they *still* not achieving their goals? Because they are missing the second key to a breakthrough: the power of story.

If you're not taking action and the answer is sitting right in front of you, there's only one reason: you've created a set of beliefs that you've tied into a story — a story about why it *won't* work, why it *can't* work, why it *only* works for other people. It's easy to come up with a limiting story. With a disempowering story, failure is pretty much guaranteed. This, of course, only reinforces the belief that nothing will work, and so the cycle continues.

Know Your Money Story

We all develop a unique relationship with money in terms of how we acquire it, how we use it and how we manage it. This relationship is developed from the messages we receive during childhood about money and values, and how our brain integrates that information at the time.

A money story is typically a collection of thoughts, beliefs and attitudes we have about money. Like a movie script tells an actor what to say and how to behave in each scene, a money story dictates what you say and what you think around money.

Most conflict over money is really a collision of so-called *money messages*. They are the direct and indirect messages we receive as we grow up and those messages we see regularly in print or electronic media, often from advertising. We take in the message and we process and synthesize that information based on our understanding of the world and life at that time. The result is often an oversimplified interpretation that is not true *in* all situations, but which may be applied *to* all situations. The tricky part of discovering your money stories is that while some reside in your conscious mind, many exist just below the surface in your subconscious. Both types of money stories impact your financial decision making on a daily basis.

Our families of origin are the primary source of money messages, but religion, school, friends and extended family, and society are also delivering messages regularly. Let's look closer at a few of those sources.

Your culture impacts your beliefs about money and its purpose. People raised in the United States are raised with consumer-driven messages of consumption, luxury, and the idea that the person with the most toys wins. Other cultures have messaging opposite of this, which focus more on a person's contribution to society. We apply unconscious meaning to any given thing via the culture(s) in which we are raised. While it's obvious that cultures are different from one another, what most people don't realize is that *these differences actually lead to our processing the same information in different ways.*

Take for instance, your *family history*. This is how your parents and caregivers handled financial matters during your childhood, your level of awareness of it, and the emotional responses to money and financial matters you may have received directly or indirectly. Research shows that your money personality is primarily formed by the age of fourteen, which highlights just how influential these years are on your money mindset.

Your personal financial experiences, whether viewed as positive or negative have an impact on your money mindset. Significant life events such as receiving a sizeable inheritance, divorce or being laid off leave a lasting mark. Each of these events usually brings mixed emotions that must be understood and eventually integrated into your mindset.

Economic social class. The economic social class you were born into also influences your money mindset. I would also add for those living cross culturally or raising so-called third country kids to think about the economic social class you think you are in versus the class you're in because of your relocation and what conflicting messages the kids may receive. Your economic class often provides a different perspective on money and its purpose.

Gender. Traditionally, and I believe this is global and across cultures, boys are raised to be competitive, to be good providers in adulthood and therefore to make money. Although the traditional roles are shifting, girls are typically raised to be caregivers and to help others while putting their needs, monetary and others, second.

Age. This is about your generation and what major world or country-level events occurred during your childhood that colors your perspective on money and wealth. For example, people who grew up during the Great Depression in the United States or the two world wars have strong ideas about money, survival, and saving. In contrast, the so-called Baby Boom generation raised in a post-war expansion period saw the price of real estate skyrocket over their lifetime and indoctrinated the idea of traditional pension plans and traditional retirement. Generations X and Y have experienced even more conflicting messages.

Religion. Religion and money seem to have an interesting, often conflicting, relationship. No matter what your religious upbringing or current affiliation is, religion has a direct bearing on your money stories. One area of influence is that of wealth versus poverty. In certain religions it's noble to be poor, while in another, the accumulation of wealth itself is not evil as long as it is used wisely.

Some examples of messages you may have heard during your lifetime are: "taking risks is bad"; "money brings happiness"; "if you love money, don't tell anyone"; "the only safe investment is land"; "I don't deserve money"; "women don't belong in business"; "money only comes from hard work" and "more money will make things better."

Sometimes money stories translate to power. For example, I worked with a couple we referred to a specialist. In this situation, one spouse worked outside the home and controlled how the money was spent, while the other worked in the home and deferred to the other spouse's decisions. The resulting messaging (to the children and everyone else) was that money determines who has the power and control in the family. Therefore, the spouse who earns less money must agree with the decisions of the one who earns more. This created a set of expectations around how partners carry out their roles when it comes to money.

Disagreements are not always related to how we earn, spend or manage our money. They can also extend to how we teach, directly or indirectly, money concepts to children.

In another situation, the subject of allowance came up in conversation during a meeting with a client couple. The issue was a disagreement about how to handle the fact that their son kept running out of his allowance. They wanted to help their child learn to better manage his money. One partner wanted a tracking sheet prepared each week and also wanted to initiate a fine when the tracking sheet was not prepared. The other partner felt that the lack of tracking was as important an issue but vehemently disagreed with the penalty. It turned out that one partner had received an allowance as a child and learned firsthand about the quality of the choices made, whereas the other partner had grown up in a family that could not afford to provide an allowance and subsequently that partner valued self-sufficiency. *This disagreement was more about competing values than about the child's spending habits or the lack of tracking.*

Understanding and possibly reframing our *life + wealth beliefs* is a critical step toward building a healthier relationship with money.

To successfully change your relationship with money, you should identify your money stories and understand how each one impacts your life. Once you are aware of these money messages you can then decide whether to listen to them or not. Until you identify these beliefs, making lasting changes in your financial habits will be challenging.

So what stories have you been telling yourself about money? Do you believe that you're not earning enough income to put anything aside? Maybe your story is "I'm just not good with numbers" or that "being in service to others is more important than making a lot of money." I have a tool to help you identify some of your messages and stories. It's a workbook titled *Uncover Your Money Beliefs* and you can download it from the book resources vault at your leisure.

Sometimes money stories tie directly to our self-worth. I fell into this situation early in my career. I took the fiduciary code of "put the interests of your clients ahead of yourself" to heart. It was great at first. I felt good. But at some point, I realized that I was sabotaging my own success. I undercharged for my time and paid my key staff more than I paid myself. I realized later that a couple of things were going on. The first stemmed from my childhood and from my involvement at the international certification level of my profession. One of the stories playing out was that Wall Street is all about greed. I wanted to prove this story wrong. I was employed as a stockbroker but self-identified as a financial planner and offered financial planning services in addition to stock trading. Still, the more money I made in brokerage services versus the financial planning services, the more guilt I felt. I also started to hear this play out socially. One of the first Initial Public Offerings I sold allowed my husband and me to pay $25,000 for our first car, in cash. That didn't go without being noticed by friends and my family back in the United States. The response was not what I was expecting. I received disdain from some and social invitations from others who were not really my friends before the IPO. I felt stuck in the middle of two worlds, which triggered a whole other set of internal conflicts bringing me back to my childhood where I grew up between two completely different financial worlds: financial struggle on one side and the upper middle class on the other. Suddenly the whole reason I went into the profession in the first place was facing me head-on. It triggered deeper emotional issues—it brought back self-esteem challenges and I was reminded of the world I thought I'd left behind, which brought up messages like, "who do you think you are?" and "you're no better than any of us."

I reevaluated. I created a new story: a belief that said you can do well but only so well or else people will judge you. If you stand out and do *too* well financially, your current friends and family won't like you and the other people, those "Wall Street types," will drag you over to the "dark side."

For a few years, I did well in my life and business but my income didn't grow significantly. I was earning just enough to be comfortable. Until I hit a tipping point, a point where I thought, *this is ridiculous. If I can expand and give more knowledge to help more people, why not? If I can expand my ability to give, why not?* I then learned more about money messages and money stories and I discovered that I had a deep-seated fear that people would judge me. I wanted to please everyone so I made it okay to do more for others and make other people money, but *I* wasn't allowed the same success I provided my clients. I was sabotaging my own personal success. Like so many others, I told myself that making money was wrong, that it couldn't serve, that it isn't spiritual. But I ultimately came back to the more positive ideal I started my career with — that if you become an asset in other people's lives, you are blessed in many ways and money is only one of them. I came to understand that being successful is how we perpetuate the doing of the good. It's how we serve others. It's like the airline announcements to place your mask on before assisting others.

I had to hit that threshold where I was tired of trying to please everyone. I had to accept that my whole life—having come from the ninety percent—I aspired to be a part of the ten percent of people who were making a difference *and* enjoying life. But I stayed in the ninety percent to fit in. Once I understood my familial and cultural influences, I had to shift my story to one that embraced a way to stop playing small and to earn more, in the same way that I strove to give more, contribute more and love more.

With that shift in belief, strategies and a clear path appeared. The truth is, they were there all along I was simply blind to them. I couldn't see them until I shifted my mindset. I can tell you from experience and training: when you get rid of your limiting stories, find the strategies that work, and take action, the results are truly miraculous.

Sometimes money stories cause additional challenges, like my Upper Limit Problem, where I was restricting my financial growth, thinking it was diminishing the work I should be doing for others, or it was wrong for me to be successful.

To quote Gay Hendricks, the author of *The Big Leap*, "each of us has an inner thermostat setting that determines how much love, success, and creativity we allow ourselves to enjoy. When we exceed our inner thermostat setting, we will often do something to sabotage ourselves, causing us to drop back into the old, familiar zone where we feel secure."

According to Gay, our thermostat setting, as she calls it, is usually programmed in early childhood. In childhood, our Upper Limit Problem develops in acts of misguided altruism. She writes: "Specifically, it develops with our attempts to take care of the feelings of others. Children are uncommonly skilled at reading body language. Perhaps you notice that the smile disappears from your mother's face when you outshine one of your siblings. You quickly learn to pull back a little from shining to take care of your mother's feelings. Many years later in adult life, you may find the very same pattern operating even though there is no mother around whose feelings you need to protect." The issue of the upper limit is if you make a leap in one area of your life, such as money, your Upper Limit Problem quickly triggers guilt that keeps you from enjoying your new abundance.

Guilt operates in conjunction with the Upper Limit Problem. It shows up when we're feeling good about something, we're making progress, or we're about to breakthrough to another level. When we're feeling good, we may come up against a story or belief such as "I must not feel good, because fundamentally flawed people like me don't deserve it." Guilt is the result of these two powerful forces clashing with one another. When the belief or story clashes with the positive feelings you're enjoying, one of them has to win. If the belief wins, you turn down the volume on the positive feeling or lose some money or start an intimacy or money-destroying argument with your partner. If the good feeling wins, then congratulations! Your practice in expanding your capacity for positive energy is paying off.

This capacity for positive energy expands in small increments each time you consciously let yourself enjoy the money you have, the love you feel and the creativity you express in the world. As that capacity for enjoyment expands, so does your financial abundance, the love you feel, and the creativity you express.

Take a moment to appreciate how radical this idea is. Most people think they'll finally feel good when they have more money, better relationships, and more creativity. I understand this point of view, because I felt the same way until I realized that was my parents' story.

What a powerful moment it is, though, when we finally see that we have it the wrong way around. We can all find and nurture the capacity for positive feelings *now*, rather than waiting until some longed-for event occurs.

11

CROSS-BORDER LIFE + WEALTH INFORMATION MANAGEMENT

Planning is important but you need the right information before you can run analysis, "what-if scenarios" and make decisions. In this chapter, we'll get you and your data organized, and we'll cover some basic banking issues including credit, establishing bank accounts, currency exchange and the emergency fund. We'll also look at foreign bank and financial asset reporting issues that affect those of us with connections to the United States.

Getting Organized

Record keeping is an important element of organizing your finances. Thanks to the wonders of technology, keeping financial records doesn't have to be difficult.

Depending on your circumstances, you may have reporting requirements to more than one country. Each partner may have different requirements regarding the information to provide, in addition to overlapping requirements. For example, some countries allow deductions for charitable gifts. If you claim such a gift on your tax return, you'll want to have records to prove it. Entering that information in your electronic bookkeeping system without supporting documentation will not convince a revenue agent if you are audited. Some common sense in this area can go a long way. Keep documents and receipts for transactions that may be important in the future. For example, grocery receipts showing what you purchased this week probably do not have much use to you in the future; however, confirmation receipts of online payments to life insurance and other policies could be very useful if a dispute were to arise.

Setting up files. Organizing personal finances is probably one of the most common items on the perpetual to-do list. It's exactly the sort of thing that you mean to do but never get around to. It stands to reason, that the more mobile you are, the lower the likelihood that you have all your important papers organized into an easy-to-use filing system. Unfortunately, as you'll see as we move into more of the technical areas of cross-border financial planning, the more mobile you are, the more organized you need to be.

I recommend keeping original documents in a safety deposit box. I suggest you save a copy of these originals and store them in appropriately labeled files with your other important papers. The files are best organized in a safe, virtual (aka cloud) environment such as a paid version of Dropbox, the personal edition of Box, Microsoft One Drive, Apple iCloud or Google Drive. Each partner should have access to the folders in the virtual environment.

I also recommend you create a list of passwords and online accounts and keep them in a safe location. Each partner should know the location and have access to this document.

If you have young adult children, consider adding their information to this list in case of emergency. Also consider allowing them their own folder on the virtual drive. They most likely have a bank account or at a minimum an account that is joint with a parent. Getting into the habit of saving electronic statements and scanning or taking a photo of hard copy statements and saving them to the virtual drive will teach them some important financial life skills *and* help you keep them organized.

This virtual drive can also serve as a place to keep your important financial receipts for the year. This virtual filing cabinet will keep you organized throughout the year and provide the information you need when it's time to prepare your tax returns.

A common question I often get, is how do I organize the folders? My preference is one folder labeled Legal. This would contain copies of passports, wills, trust documents, immigration paperwork, loan documents, insurance policies and agreements. And another folder labeled Medical to hold key medical history information, and then one folder for each year. In this folder you may have subfolders for bank statements, investment account statements, retirement plan statements, taxes (e.g., estimated tax vouchers and receipts, plus a copy of what was filed when complete), bills and certain receipts.

Check out the Resources section at the back of the book for a link to *The Expat Family File*. It's a resource that can help you make sure you know what to look for and stay organized.

Banking and Credit

These two tactical issues are highly dependent on your location independent plan. They require you to think in the longer term to inform the short term.

Keeping bank accounts in one jurisdiction may keep you resident in that location but consider the implications of closing everything down in one location before you have anything set up in the other location where you may not have any credit and don't know all the logistical issues you may face.

Some strategies you might want to consider include:

- Research local banks in your new host or home country. Use any pre-visits or house-hunting trips to inquire at local banks about services for foreign nationals and non-permanent residents.

- Check into foreign exchange requirements. For example, if you're moving to India, you'll need to understand the specifics of the exchange control legislation currently in place. The definition of residential status of individuals under the exchange control law differs from the definition under the Income Tax Act, 1961.[14]

- Do not automatically assume that if you already bank with a global bank, that banking in your host country will be the same as banking at home. Most often, banks are subject to local restrictions and may require different procedures than you are accustomed to at home.

- Few banks will accept telephone instructions for funds transfers because they can't verify the identity of the caller and will not authorize the transfer unless they are face to face with the customer and can verify the customer's identification and signature.

- Check to see if there are any transactional limits on account to account transfers, bill payments or wire transfers.

Keep in mind that online banking is usually country specific and will provide service for where your accounts are domiciled. This means that online banking in the U.S. may only provide service for your U.S. bank accounts and not any bank accounts held overseas. The bill payment function is usually also country specific. In this regard, you will probably find that you can't use the bill payment facility to pay a bill outside of that jurisdiction.

Credit. One of the more challenging aspects of cross-border living is that your credit history does not travel with you.

From a banking perspective, foreign nationals new to a country without a credit or work history in the country are generally viewed as more of a risk than local customers. While some countries have established credit bureaus and can provide their citizens with a credit history, a foreign credit history does not usually transfer across

---

[14] For answers to Frequently Asked Questions visit the Reserve Bank of India's consumer page: http://www.rbi.org.in/scripts/FEMA_FAQs.aspx

countries, and most banks are not familiar with how to interpret a foreign credit report. As a result, an expatriate new to a country, and applying for credit, such as a credit card, may experience difficulties.

If you're moving to a new country for more permanent reasons, you'll want to look into the various options that might be available to you for transferring credit. If your current bank has a branch in the country where you want to or need to establish credit, investigate if it can provide documentation or some other type of information that the other branch will accept as a starting place.

Currency Speculation by Default

When your family goals involve more than one country, it's natural to take a truly global investment view. But when you invest in markets around the world, the currency in which your holdings are denominated can have a significant impact on portfolio returns. Fluctuations in exchange rates can reduce, or enhance, investment returns.

In many situations in cross-border financial planning, and for varying reasons, there may be several different investment portfolios in different accounts under several ownership options. For instance, life insurance, trusts, joint ownership, tax-deferred. If this is the case for you, it is important to match your currency and investments to the liabilities to be funded by the given account.

For example, suppose that you live in the United Kingdom and are planning to relocate in fifteen years to a property you own in France. If the portfolio that is to provide income to you while living in France during the remainder of your lifetime is presently held in UK Pounds Sterling or U.S. Dollars, the exchange rate at payout will affect your purchasing power. You may wish to structure the portfolio so the base currency is the Euro and look to the other currencies in the name of diversification.

Similarly, the objective of a trust plays a key role in the selection of currency. For example, if the same UK resident is placing assets into trust for the benefit of his or her children, who are residents of the United States, then it may be desirable for the trust to have U.S. dollars as its base currency.

While no one can predict the future movement of currency exchange rates, there are ways for you to manage the risk that comes with cross-border investing. Be clear about your intentions, if currency is part of your overall strategy. For instance, if the goal is long-term (e.g., you plan on retiring abroad or purchasing a property or business in another country, or sending children to college), converting into investments denominated in the foreign currency over time can help reduce potential currency exchange risk. By gradually converting, you'll average out your cost and avoid a situation in which you may have to convert your savings when the exchange rate is least in your favor. Additionally, the matching must occur in relation to the timeline of the goal.

If the goal is to protect an investment portfolio that invests in financial assets via multiple currencies and whose performance is being reported in a single currency, and you expect that the withdrawals from that portfolio will be in the reported currency, then you may want to consider hedging the currency risk here. But first I would ask why the portfolio is invested that way in the first place. This could be a situation where you're hoping that tactical shifts will overcome a potentially flawed strategy or a strategy that is simply to outperform a benchmark and the achievement of one or more specific goals is a byproduct. The other issue of currency can occur when you terminate residence in one country, leaving nothing in that country that needs to be funded, with no plans of return and you want all your money to be denominated in the currency of your new location.

Overall the question to be answered is how sensitive is your situation to currency risk? Your *Cross-Border Life + Wealth Achievement Plan* provides the guidance for your decision making because without it important decisions may be driven by emotions or clever marketing and not necessarily sound reasoning.

We've already discussed the Money Inventory tool. This tool helps you determine the flow of funds for a given country and/or currency. Once all decisions are made through the alignment sub process you arrive at one or more spending plans. As you may have already discovered, the action required to carry out the spending plan(s) often includes transfers between countries or accounts in different currencies. As a reminder, this is typically the case when you may have rent or some other income source paying in to an account in the currency covered by a spending plan, but rent alone is not sufficient to cover all the expenses identified in that plan.

The cost of currency conversion (the rate charged by the bank or other intermediary) and wire transfers can add up to large sums very quickly. I often see that people underestimate these costs and they rarely make their way into spending plans without prompting. It can be very expensive to set up regular recurring transfers that are more frequent than quarterly. When we're building the cash management portion of a *Cross-Border Life + Wealth Achievement Plan*, I typically like to see if there is a way an account can be funded and replenished once or twice per year.

Create an Emergency Fund

A high priority in any sound financial plan is to protect yourself and your family from unexpected financial emergencies by maintaining a reserve of funds that can be accessed if needed. Financial emergencies might include replacement of an appliance, a short-term disability that causes you to miss several weeks or months of work, serious illness, and evacuation — in short just about any unforeseen event or expense. The emergency fund is a key financial tool to be incorporated into the cross-border financial plan. The appropriate amount of money to hold in an emergency fund depends primarily on the stability of your income, spending patterns, your access to credit, and stability of the banking system in your host or home country. For internationally mobile people, all three of these factors are variables that must be assessed in the context of your *Cross-Border Life + Wealth Achievement Plan.*

If you've put the necessary effort into the crafting of a thoughtful spending plan, then you have most of the information you need to determine an appropriate amount of funds to hold in the account(s) that serve as your emergency fund. Total your fixed expenses and those variable expenses that must be covered by your income. You should be using annual figures. Funds allocated to your spending plan for things like vacation, hobbies and most (if not all) luxury items should *not* be included in these totals. At a minimum you will want three months' worth of expenses. In many cases, we've suggested the equivalent of six or even twelve months, if possible.

Typically, you'll want to ensure that the currency in which the emergency fund is invested matches the currency of your home base. In certain cases, where you are managing more than one residence in countries with different currencies, it may make sense to have more than one emergency fund. In certain cases, we have set up an emergency fund to accompany a given spending plan currency.

Using Your Organized Financial Information

Although this section of this chapter will look at some of the tax and procedural rules that apply to individuals and families with connections to the United States, the issues raised may be relevant to nationals of other countries.

Foreign Bank and Financial Asset Reporting

Although it's perfectly legal for U.S. persons to have foreign bank accounts and assets around the world, the U.S. government wants to know about those accounts. Although we are focused on rules specific for U.S. citizens and residents here, it is important to note that other governments have also enacted similar reporting requirements including the United Kingdom and Canada.

As far as the U.S. tax law is concerned, U.S. citizens and permanent residents are required to report any income from foreign bank and financial accounts or assets. The fact that the income is not reported to the IRS on an information return does not alter the legal duty of the U.S. citizen/resident.

The Bank Secrecy Act (BSA) gives the Treasury Department authority to collect information from U.S. persons who have financial interests in or signature authority over financial accounts maintained with financial institutions located outside of the U.S. A provision of the BSA requires that a Form 114, Report of Foreign Bank and Financial Accounts (FBAR, previously known as Form TD F 90-22.1) be filed with the Financial Crimes Enforcement Network (FinCEN, a bureau of the Treasury Department) if the aggregate maximum values of the foreign financial accounts that you have a financial interest in or signature authority over, exceed $10,000 at any time during the calendar year.

Enforcement authority regarding the FBAR has been delegated to IRS, which can impose penalties for noncompliance. Penalties for willful failures to file an FBAR can be as high as $100,000 or 50% of the value of the unreported account. The report is filed separately from your income tax return and can only be filed electronically. For tax years after 2015, Form 114 must be filed by April 15 of the year following the tax year; however, an extension is allowed until October 15 of the year following the tax year, provided that you meet the requirements.

An often overlooked issue is the completion of Part III of Schedule B to Form 1040, where your foreign accounts and assets may dictate that this schedule be filed even though you do not have any interest or dividends to report.

Form 8938, Statement of Specified Foreign Financial Assets may also be required if the value of your foreign financial assets exceeds certain thresholds.

What is IRS Form 8938?

Form 8938 is the Statement of Specified Foreign Financial Assets. It is another way for the U.S. government to gather information about the financial activities of U.S. citizens and residents of the United States. All taxpayers with accounts and certain assets outside of the United States should review the instructions and thresholds to understand their individual obligations.

Who Should File Form 8938?

Form 8938 requires U.S. citizens and residents of the United States who have foreign financial assets over a certain value to report this information to the IRS. These financial assets include bank accounts as well as brokerage accounts, the stock or securities of foreign issuers, and foreign financial instruments. Also on the list are foreign-issued life insurance or annuity contracts with a cash value, retirement accounts and shares in foreign hedge funds and private equity funds. The thresholds are as follows:

	If the total value on the last day of the tax year is above:	If the total value at any time during the tax year is above:
Unmarried and living in the USA	$50,000	$75,000
Married, filing jointly, and living in the USA	$100,000	$150,000
Married, filing seperately, living in the USA	$50,000	$75,000
Unmarried and living abroad	$200,000	$300,000
Married, filing jointly, and living abroad	$400,000	$600,000
Married, filing seperately, living abroad	$200,000	$300,000

How Do I File Form 8938?

File IRS Form 8938 with your tax return. The 8938 is subject to the same deadlines and extensions as the rest of your return.

Reporting for Non-U.S. Trusts and Gifts from Non-U.S. Persons and Entities

U.S. citizens and residents of the United States are required to report gifts that exceed USD 100,000 that are received from any non-U.S. individual or estate. Similarly, you are also required to report any amount received from a foreign corporation or foreign partnership that are treated as gifts rather than some form of income if that amount is more than USD 15,797 in 2017.

Generally, if you are the settlor or the beneficiary of a non-U.S. trust, certain information will be required on Form 3520, *Annual Return to Report Transactions with Foreign Trusts and Receipt of Certain Foreign Gifts*. When you create a foreign trust or transfer property to a foreign trust, this form is required to be filed within ninety days of the creation or transfer. In addition, you may also be responsible for seeing that the trust files Form 3520-A, *Annual Information Return of Foreign Trust with a U.S. Owner*.

Although the reporting for this form can be very complicated, it doesn't mean you need to panic or find ways to exclude yourself or other U.S. persons from this situation. There are experts with sufficient experience in this area you can consult. If you're told to avoid the risks of being associated with non-U.S. trusts ask why. It's important to understand the rules so you can make a good decision.

Foreign Currency Exchange Rules

A common area of confusion relates to the reporting of income, deductions and asset values that are not denominated in U.S. dollars, on both tax returns and information reporting forms. When you save important information, such as receipts for expenses relating to an investment property you own overseas, you will also need to obtain currency exchange information to ensure the correct value is reported. This is the case because you must report your income and deductions (and asset values) in U.S. dollars. Thus income and expenses paid in a currency other than U.S. dollars should generally be converted to U.S. dollars using the exchange rate at the date of receipt or the date of payment, although under some circumstances it may be appropriate to use an average exchange rate for the year. When you calculate your capital gains and losses, you must use historical exchange rates. This could result in an outcome in U.S. dollar terms that is different than in the currency in which the sale took place. Let's look at an example:

Rita purchased 100 common shares of stock in a British corporation for GBP 15 per share, when the exchange rate was GBP 1.00 = USD 1.60. Three years later, she sold the stock for GBP 20 per share, at a time when the exchange rate was GBP 1.00 = USD 1.20. So, Rita purchased her shares for GBP 1,500, and sold them for GBP 2,000, a gain of GBP 500. However, for U.S. tax purposes, Rita will be treated as having received USD 1,200 for shares she paid USD 1,600 for, realizing a capital loss of USD 400.

U.S. Tax Return due Dates and Extensions

U.S. citizens and residents must generally file their tax returns by April 15, but if you are resident abroad on that date, you get an automatic extension of two months to June 15. (You may also want to note that any due date that falls on a Saturday, Sunday or holiday is also extended to the next weekday that is not a holiday.)

If you qualify for this automatic extension, there is no special form to file, but you should attach a statement to your tax return explaining that you qualify for the automatic two-month extension.

If more time is needed to prepare your tax return, you can get an extension to October 15 by filing Form 4868, *Application for Automatic Extension of Time to File U.S. Individual Income Tax Return*. For the extension to be valid, you must file Form 4868 by the tax return due date (e.g. generally April 15 or June 15 as mentioned earlier in this section), and you must make a reasonable estimate of your tax liability.

A special extension is available if you need more time to meet the time requirements to claim the Foreign Earned Income Exclusion (see the next chapter for a discussion of these time requirements). You aren't allowed to claim the Foreign Earned Income Exclusion in your tax return until you actually qualify for it, and in many cases this can mean waiting a full year to file your tax return. In this situation you would file Form 2350, *Application for Extension of Time to File U.S. Income Tax Return*, by the due date of your return (again, April 15 or June 15, depending on your situation). In most situations, the latest date the tax return can be extended to is January 30 of the year following the original due date.

Keep in mind that tax return extensions are not extensions of time to pay tax due. Any tax paid after April 15 will be subject to interest and potentially penalties, even if the return filing date has been extended. Thus if you anticipate owing tax with your tax return, you should pay it by April 15.

Voluntary Compliance Programs

You may have read to this point and are now wondering if your reporting was truly accurate. Or you may be thinking you might have left out one or more forms in one or more years. The most important thing you can do if that is the case is to make getting this all straightened out a priority. After all you really cannot engage in creating much of a financial plan if you haven't taken care of your obligations.

The IRS has made modifications over the past several years to the programs that allow for late reporting of previously undisclosed non-U.S. assets and generally getting current. At the same time, the IRS continually reaffirms its commitment to cracking down on U.S. taxpayer compliance.

At the time of this writing, the Internal Revenue Service offers four options to address these issues. The programs are summarized here; however, I have provided links to the location where additional details are found for each program. The specific facts and circumstances of your situation will need to be evaluated against eligibility, potential penalties and any risks presented to arrive at an appropriate option.

The two most significant programs are the Offshore Voluntary Disclosure Program (OVDP) and the Streamlined Procedures for those resident in the United States (Streamlined Domestic Offshore Procedures) and those residing overseas (Streamlined Foreign Offshore Procedures).

The OVDP is generally designed for those who are concerned that their failure to report income and failure to disclose foreign financial accounts might be viewed by the IRS as willful and who wish to avoid potential criminal penalties. The IRS began an open-ended OVDP in 2012 following strong interest in the first two programs. The current modified program is referred to as the 2014 OVDP. As with all of the programs, eight years of tax and reporting documentation is required.

For more information visit:
https://www.irs.gov/individuals/international-taxpayers/offshore-voluntary-disclosure-program-frequently-asked-questions-and-answers-2012-revised.

The Streamlined Filing Compliance Procedures can generally be used if you failed to report foreign financial assets and pay the required tax due from the unreported asset, and can certify that this conduct was not willful. In addition, you cannot be under a civil examination or a criminal investigation by the IRS. Generally, three years of tax returns and related information returns plus six years of FBARs are required. Under the Streamlined Foreign Offshore procedures, previously unpaid taxes must be paid with interest but the failure-to-file and failure-to-pay penalties, accuracy-related penalties, information return penalties and FBAR penalties are waived. The Streamlined Domestic Offshore procedures impose a 5% penalty called a miscellaneous offshore penalty on certain foreign financial assets.

The following links may be of additional help:

- Overview of the Procedures:

    - https://www.irs.gov/individuals/international-taxpayers/streamlined-filing-compliance-procedures

- FAQs relating to the Streamlined Foreign Offshore Procedures:

    - https://www.irs.gov/individuals/international-taxpayers/streamlined-filing-compliance-procedures-for-u-s-taxpayers-residing-outside-the-united-states-frequently-asked-questions-and-answers

- FAQs relating to the Streamlined Domestic Offshore Procedures:

    - https://www.irs.gov/individuals/international-taxpayers/streamlined-filing-compliance-procedures-for-u-s-taxpayers-residing-in-the-united-states-frequently-asked-questions-and-answers

Delinquent FBAR Submission Procedures. U.S. citizens and residents who don't need either the OVDP or the Streamlined Filing Compliance Procedures but who have not filed a required Report of Foreign Bank and Financial Accounts (FBAR) (FinCEN Form 114, previously Form TD F 90-222.1), have not already been contacted by the IRS about the FBAR(s) and are not under a civil examination or criminal investigation by the IRS should consider filing the late FBARs electronically at FinCEN using the BSA E-filing System (https://bsaefiling. fincen.treas.gov/main.html) and include a statement explain why the FBAR(s) were filed late. For more information on this option visit: https://www.irs.gov/individuals/international-taxpayers/delinquent-fbar-submission-procedures.

The *Delinquent International Information Return Submission Procedures* offer an easy process for those who don't need to use the OVDP or Streamlined Procedures to file late or amended tax returns to report and pay additional tax, but who: (1) have not filed one or more required international information returns; (2) have reasonable cause for not timely filing the information returns, and of course, are not under a civil examination or a criminal investigation and have not already been contacted about the information returns, by the IRS. Under these procedures, the information returns must be filed with a statement of all facts establishing reasonable cause for the failure to file. More details can be obtained from:
https://www.irs.gov/individuals/international-taxpayers/delinquent-international-information-return-submission-procedures.

12

U.S. INCOME & ESTATE TAXATION OF U.S. CITIZENS AND RESIDENTS

Taxes are the price we pay for civilization.
— Oliver Wendell Holmes, Jr.

International taxation is one of the core areas in cross-border financial planning to be analyzed and understood. Although this chapter will provide some examples of international taxation remember, as with all the examples in this book, they are not prescriptive nor are they complete. They provide context and an increased level of understanding of the issues involved in cross-border financial planning. Formal professional advice must be sought in this and all other specialized areas.

Finally before we move deeper into issues and rules that affect U.S. citizens and residents, it is important to note that significant revisions to the tax law were made as a result of the 2017 Tax Act, commonly referred to as the "Tax Cuts and Jobs Act of 2017," which came into being at the time of publication. Thus, while there may be references in specific areas that are affected, the information reflects the rules as they apply to taxable years ending on or before December 31, 2017. You should use this information only as an educational tool to assist in the recognition of issues and to aid your discussion with professionals.

U.S. citizens, non-U.S. citizens who are resident in the Unites States and U.S. Permanent Resident card (aka Green Card) holders are taxed on worldwide income, with certain exclusions, and are required to meet any other reporting obligations, *regardless* of where they reside in the world.

If you are born abroad but have a U.S. Certificate of Birth Abroad, you are most likely a dual national of the country in which you were born *and* the United States. Not having a passport issued by the United States does not mean that you are not a U.S. citizen and therefore are not subject to the rules and issues highlighted in this book. The reality is that you are. There is some relief for you should you not wish to remain a citizen of the United States in the form of specific exceptions to the exit tax.

Additionally, in the year that you move to or from the United States, your tax situation may be particularly challenging and therefore it is generally advisable to seek assistance prior to relocation.

Here we'll cover a few of the more common areas where misinformation and confusion is typically found.

Taxation of Foreign Earnings

The compensation you receive for services that you perform in a country other than the United States is generally referred to as foreign earnings. This is not to be confused with the idea that "foreign" means anything other than your current location of residence. This is often most confusing to U.S. citizens born abroad, who do not know or understand this distinction. On a related note, only the location where the services are provided determines whether earned income is foreign — the nationality of the employer, the location of the bank account into which the earnings were paid, and the currency in which the earnings were paid are *not* relevant. The exception here is that amounts paid by the United States or its agencies to government employees or members of the U.S. armed services are not considered to be foreign earned income. Similarly, income earned working in Puerto Rico or U.S. possessions is not considered to be foreign earned income although other tax benefits may be available.

Earned income is not restricted to wages and includes bonus income, commissions, cost-of-living allowances and incentives, tax reimbursements, lodging and/or housing allowance, home leave and educational reimbursements or allowances and moving expense reimbursements. Also, an amount is considered income whether it's paid directly to you or paid on your behalf, and whether it's paid in cash or as a benefit-in-kind. Determining the earned income to report is often a challenge when you work for a foreign employer who does not provide you with a Form W-2 and who may not be familiar with the rules for reporting income to the United States. Therefore it is up to you to understand how this works. You're still required to provide the correct information whether you self-prepare your tax return or work with a professional.

Two other issues are relevant here. First, if you work in both the United States and in a foreign country (or countries), your earned income has to be allocated between U.S. and foreign source income based on the number of days worked in each location during the year. The exception is that some earned income, such as foreign housing allowance, may be considered exclusively a foreign source. The second issue is timing. We must distinguish between when the foreign earned income was physically earned versus when we received it. This is important for purposes of the Foreign Earned Income Exclusion (FEIE), which we will look at in more depth, because the FEIE for the current year is used to offset foreign earned income that was earned in the current year.

The Foreign Earned Income Exclusion (FEIE)

If you establish that you have a tax home in a foreign country and meet either the bona fide residence test or the physical presence test, you're entitled to claim the Foreign Earned Income Exclusion and if you have more foreign earned income than the maximum allowable FEIE, you may also be able to claim the housing cost exclusion. The value of the exclusion is adjusted annually for inflation and the housing cost exclusion is available if your qualified housing costs exceed 16% of the maximum FEIE, up to maximum housing costs of 30% of the maximum FEIE. The 30% limit is increased for certain locations around the world. The specific values and limits for each year are widely published and may be found in the instructions to IRS Form 2555, Foreign Earned Income.

The foreign earned income and housing cost exclusions are elective, *not* automatic. This means that if you qualify to claim the exclusions, you can choose whether or not to do so. That said, once you've claimed the exclusions in a tax return, you have effectively elected to claim the exclusions in *all* future years that you qualify to claim them. You can choose to *not* claim the exclusions after having claimed them in an earlier year by revoking the election; however, when you do this you will not be able to make the election again for six years, unless you obtain special permission from the IRS. You make the election to claim either or both exclusion by completing Form 2555, Foreign Earned Income and attaching it to your tax return.

Because of the interaction between the stacking rule, which I will describe later, and the foreign tax credit, it's possible that there are situations when it's not beneficial to claim the foreign earned income exclusion. Generally, this is more likely if you are paying tax in a country that has higher tax rates than the United States. Calculations will be required to determine the impact to future years by the revocation against the benefit of a lower tax liability in the current year, and may be beneficial if made *prior* to making the election.

Families with Two Income Earners

If you are married, both you and your spouse can claim the foreign earned income exclusion, but each of you must qualify separately and if either spouse has any unused exclusion, the other cannot use it.

Additionally, if you come from a community property state, community property law is generally disregarded when determining the amount of your foreign earned income.

If you and your spouse live together, housing costs can be shared by both of you, or allocated to one or the other, whichever is more beneficial.

Qualifying for the Elections

To qualify to claim the foreign earned income exclusion, you must have foreign earned income, your tax home must be in a foreign country, and you must meet one of the following tests:

• The bona fide residence test

  or

• The physical presence test

If you are a U.S. citizen, you may qualify to claim the foreign earned income exclusion and the foreign housing cost exclusion under either the bona fide residence or physical presence tests. If you are a U.S. resident alien (holder of a U.S. permanent resident card/green card) working outside the United States, in general you should use the physical presence test to qualify to claim the FEIE, although, if you are a citizen of a country that has an income tax treaty with the United States, you may be allowed to use the bona fide residence test to qualify to claim the foreign earned income exclusion. We'll look at those tests in more detail, but first it's crucial to understand the concept of the foreign tax home.

Foreign Tax Home

The term "tax home" generally means the location of your regular or principal place of business or employment. It's where you are permanently or indefinitely engaged to work as an employee or self-employed individual. Having a tax home in a given location doesn't necessarily mean that the given location is your residence or domicile for tax purposes. The location of your tax home often depends on whether your assignment is temporary or indefinite. If the employment exceeds one year in a single location, it is indefinite and you will be considered to have given up your old tax home. If the assignment is expected to last a year or less the employment is considered temporary.

When a foreign assignment is taken or self-employment takes you into this realm, it's important to document factors that determine your place of abode and also indicate the intention to establish your tax home in the foreign country. Even if you meet the physical presence test, the IRS may not consider your tax home to have moved to the foreign location. However, if you satisfy the bona fide residence test, the foreign location may be considered your tax home. The IRS has issued guidelines (see Revenue Ruling 93-86) to help determine whether a work assignment away from one's regular place of employment is temporary or is indefinite. Other guidelines establish three factors for determining your place of abode, which also affects where your tax home is considered to be. The factors are:

- Whether your family accompanies you to the new location.

- Whether you duplicate living expenses by maintaining your home.

- Whether there are social or personal ties in the new location.

Although you don't necessarily have to meet all of these conditions to be considered as having moved your abode to the new location.

You aren't considered to have a tax home in a foreign country for any period in which your abode is in the United States. However, your abode is not necessarily in the United States while you are temporarily in the United States.

Bona Fide Residence Test

To use the bona fide residence test to qualify to claim the foreign earned income exclusion, your period of bona fide residence abroad must include one full calendar year. Once you meet the full-year requirement, you may also apply the bona fide residence test to the partial years abroad at the beginning and end of your assignment. Temporary visits to the United States generally will not disqualify you from claiming to be a bona fide resident of a foreign country, unless the visit to the United States is itself a period of residence in the United States.

However, you do not automatically acquire bona fide resident status by living in a foreign country for a year. Determining if you meet the test requires an analysis of all the relevant facts and circumstances. Factors that might indicate that you are a bona fide resident include:

- You purchase or lease a home in the foreign country.

- Your family makes their home in the foreign location.

- The nature of any conditions or limitations on the employment agreement, and the type and term of your visa, or your residence and/or work permit.

- Your involvement in the social life and culture of the foreign location.

It's important to note that you cannot claim that you are a nonresident of the foreign country to avoid paying resident income tax in that country and claim the bona fide residence test.

Physical Presence Test

This is a test *only* of how many days you are physically present in a foreign country. It does not depend on your intentions, the kind of residence you establish or the nature and purpose of your stay. You meet the physical presence test if you are physically present in a foreign country for 330 full days during any 12-month period. If you are claiming the FEIE for a full year, the qualifying period should be the calendar year; but for an arrival or departure year, any 12-month period that begins or ends during the tax year can be used. A day counts as a day outside the United States only if you were in one or more foreign countries for the entire 24-hour period starting at midnight. For that reason, a day of departure or arrival in a foreign country generally will not count. If you spend less than 24 hours in the United States in transit between two foreign countries, that will not be counted as physical presence in the United States.

It's important to keep detailed records of your travel while living abroad. In the year that your international assignment or residence begins or ends, the physical presence test can result in a larger pro rata FEIE than the bona fide residence test, because of the way that the 330-day requirement is applied. If you qualify to use both the bona fide residence test and the physical presence test, you may use whichever test allows the larger exclusion.

Foreign Housing Cost Exclusions

As I've already mentioned, if your foreign earned income is more than the maximum foreign earned income exclusion, you may also be able to claim the housing cost exclusion.

Qualified housing costs, are the reasonable expenses you paid (or your employer paid on your behalf) from earned income for foreign housing for you, your spouse and your dependents if they lived with you. Qualified housing expenses include rent, utilities (other than for telephone and cable television), insurance, nondeductible occupancy taxes, repairs, furniture rental and appliances, and insurance and residential parking. Mortgage interest and property tax are not considered qualified housing costs although they may be used as itemized deductions even if paid in relation to a foreign home.

Housing costs are treated slightly differently if you are self-employed.

Be Aware of the Stacking Rule and Modified Adjusted Gross Income

If you claim the foreign earned income exclusion, your income tax is figured using a special calculation called the "stacking rule," which causes the exclusions to be less beneficial than other deductions or exclusions of the same amount.

Like many countries, the United States has progressive tax rates, meaning that the higher our income, the higher the rate of tax. In the United States, each level of tax is referred to as a "bracket," with higher levels of income, or "brackets" taxed at higher tax rates.

The stacking rule causes the foreign earned income to be unique in that it offsets income that is taxed in the *lowest* brackets, rather than the *highest* brackets. It's applied by figuring the tax on taxable income without taking the foreign earned income and housing cost exclusions into account. The tax is then figured on the amount of your total foreign earned income and housing costs exclusions at the appropriate graduated tax rates and with no other deductions taken into consideration. The difference, if any, between the two amounts is your actual U.S. tax liability for the year.

Amounts excluded from gross income as a result of the foreign earned income and housing costs is added back to your Adjusted Gross Income (AGI) to calculate Modified Adjusted Gross Income, (MAGI).

This affects credits, contributions to IRAs and deductions.

Residences

A common area for financial planning attention involves the tax implications of holding, renting, or selling a principal U.S. residence. The rules that you should consider are briefly described here.

Rental Considerations

Rental income must be reported on your tax return and you can claim certain deductions against that income, including mortgage interest, property taxes, agency commissions, insurance and other operating costs of the property.

Depreciation may also be allowed on the cost of the building, improvements and furnishings left in the house, but not on the portion of the cost of the property that is attributable to land.

If rental income exceeds the deductions related to the property, the net rental income is included in taxable income. If the deductions exceed rental income, generally the net loss cannot be deducted against other ordinary income such as earned income, dividend and interest income, and active business income. The loss can be deducted against income from other rental properties and from other so-called "passive activities" such as limited partnership income. Unused losses may be carried forward to the next year and in the year the property is disposed of, any remaining loss carried forward will be fully deductible.

A special rule does allow you to deduct up to USD 25,000 of net rental loss against ordinary income if you "actively participate" in the management of the property. You actively participate if you or your spouse own at least 10% of the property and you perform management functions such as approving new tenants, approving expenditures and deciding on rental terms. This opportunity is phased out if your modified adjusted gross income (AGI after the FEIE and housing cost exclusions are added back) exceeds a certain threshold and fully disallowed at a higher threshold. These levels should be quantified before any assumption that the loss can be taken causes action.

Vacation Home Rules

If you use the property for personal purposes for more than the greater of 14 days or 10% of the number of days the home is rented during the tax year, deductions related to the rental use such as depreciation, insurance, maintenance, etc., may be limited to the amount of rental income. This means that no losses will be allowed in the current year or carried forward to a future year. It should be noted that "personal use" includes use of a property by relatives and losses may not be deducted from rental income unless a market rent is paid for use of the property. If the personal use does not exceed the 14-days/10% limitation, then the rental may instead by subject to the passive loss activity rules already mentioned.

Sale of Principal Residence

The general rule is that gain on the sale of property is taxable, including any gain on the sale of your home. However, we may qualify to exclude up to USD 250,000 (USD 500,000 for a married couple filing a joint tax return) of the gain of a principal residence assuming that we qualify for the exclusion.

Generally, the following requirements must be met:

1. You must have owned and occupied the residence as your principal residence for at least two years during the five-year period *prior* to the sale or exchange, although the two years do not have to be in one consecutive period.

2. During the two-year period ending on the date of the sale, you have not excluded gain from the sale of another home.

In certain cases, even if you don't meet the requirements for the exclusion, you may be able to claim a smaller exclusion if the primary reason you sold the home was because of a change in place of employment, health or certain other unforeseen circumstances. If you meet one of these exceptions, you may qualify for smaller maximum exclusion. You must still have owned and occupied the home as your primary residence for some period of time in the five-year period ending on the date of sale or exchange. If so, your maximum exclusion will be prorated by the ratio of the period that you did not use the home as your primary residence to two years.

For example, Peter purchased his home in New Hope, Pennsylvania, on January 1, 2016. He moved in immediately and used it as his primary residence. On May 31, 2017, he sold the home because his employer transferred him to Switzerland on a long-term assignment. Peter's maximum exclusion for gain on the sale of this home will be USD 176,813 (517 days/731 days x USD 250,000). If Peter's gain is less than USD 176,813, he can exclude the entire gain. If his gain is more than this amount, the excess will be taxed as a capital gain.

If your home had any periods of "non-qualified use" after January 1, 2009, gain attributable to the non-qualified use cannot be offset by the exclusion. Non-qualified use generally includes any period that you did not use the property as your principal residence, such as renting it out, leaving it vacant or using it as a vacation home, but only if you reoccupy the house as your primary residence afterwards.

There are two exceptions to the non-qualified use rule.

1. Periods of absence of up to ten years in the aggregate during which you or your spouse are serving on qualified official duty as a member of the uniformed services, the U.S. foreign service or the intelligence community, will not count as non-qualified use.

2. Periods of non-qualified use do not include any other period of absence, not to exceed two years in the aggregate, due to health issues, change of place of employment or certain other unforeseen circumstances.

Renting your home while you are overseas can create taxable gain on the sale of the home in another way, by creating "depreciation recapture." When you sell the property, the amount you originally paid for the property (your "basis" in the property) is decreased by the allowable depreciation deductions you took. The portion of the gain that is related to this depreciation adjustment is called depreciation recapture and cannot be offset by the exclusion for gain on the sale of a primary residence. We should also note that this depreciation recapture is taxed at 25%, rather than the 15% rate that applies to most long-term capital gains.

Foreign Properties

The rules described in this section on residences also apply to personal residences and rental properties located in foreign countries. However, special depreciation rules apply to foreign properties. These rules generally provide for longer useful lives and thus a smaller annual deduction than those allowed for domestic properties.

State Income Taxes

Tax laws vary from state to state and the connections you maintain with a state while abroad, including whether you maintain a residence there, may cause you to continue to be subject to state income tax. If you are subject to state income tax, be aware that many states do not allow the foreign earned income credit or the foreign tax credit that you might qualify for at the federal level.

Some states impose community property rules and therefore most marital income and assets are the property of both spouses, regardless of which spouse earned the income. While community property rules have no impact on couples who file a joint return, the impact on the tax liability of married couples that file separate returns can be significant. As I mentioned earlier, community property rules are not applied when calculating the foreign earned income exclusion, but it's also worth mentioning that these rules are *not* applied to the earned income of a married couple if either spouse is a nonresident alien.

The Passive Foreign Investment Company (PFIC)

The laws involving PFICs are complex and not very well known by a large percentage of U.S. citizens and residents, as well as many advisors and tax professionals. We'll touch on a few of high-level concepts; however, the goal is awareness not details. As with all of the content in this section of the book, guidance will need to be sought.

First, let's understand what a PFIC is. A passive foreign investment company is generally defined as a foreign corporation in which 75% or more of its income is passive, or where 50% or more of its assets are passive or are held to produce passive income. Passive income generally includes interest, dividends, rent and gains on sale.

In most cases, a pooled income fund, a unit trust, a mutual fund incorporated outside of the United States, including a money market fund are typically considered passive foreign investment companies. Be aware that foreign private equity funds, startups and holding companies can be considered PFICs.

Publicly traded mutual funds have ISIN numbers. If the fund you have invested in or are considering investing in has an ISIN that starts with letters other than "U.S." it's probably a PFIC. Just because the name sounds familiar or is identical to a mutual fund you may know exists in the United States does not mean that your foreign investment product or account is buying the U.S. version. Exchange traded funds can also have a non-U.S. version available on a non-U.S. exchange. Again, the symbol and identifying number will be different.

While there are planning strategies where the impact of PFICs can be managed, generally speaking, reportable transactions, such as income received during the year or proceeds from sale, are going be taxed under IRC Sec. 1291. Think of this treatment as being the "default rules." The specific facts and circumstances will determine how these transactions are taxed under this code section. However, we generally need to determine what portion of a distribution is "excess." The tax will be allocated to the holding period with a portion potentially being taxed at ordinary rates and/or a portion being taxed using the maximum tax rates and an interest charge. The net investment income tax applies and foreign tax credits are potentially of use.

You've probably already read about the tax treatment of the so-called "excess" portion of that transaction because that is what most people focus on, particularly those who want you to sell out their entire portfolio and move it to a U.S. custodian or at least shift into individual stocks and bonds or U.S. "situs" exchange traded funds (ETF), mutual funds or other investment vehicles. While it is true that owning PFICs in a typical investment account is not recommended, in many cases, such as foreign retirement accounts, PFICs are the only investment options and therefore it is important to know that there are two elections that if made can help avoid the unfavorable tax treatment I described above.

You can make a so-called "mark-to-market" election. If the PFIC meets eligibility and this election is timely made then gains are taxed at ordinary tax rates. It's like a pretend sale of all of your shares at the end of each year, although there are limitations on losses.

You can elect to treat the PFIC as a "qualified electing fund." If the PFIC meets eligibility and you make this election, generally you will be taxed on your share of the PFICs annual undistributed earnings. Think of the flow through as being similar to how it works with a partnership.

A partnership by itself does not meet the definition of a PFIC. But, if a foreign partnership invests in a foreign mutual fund or other entity that meets the definition of PFIC, then the U.S. shareholders are still burdened with the related tax problems of owning a PFIC.

A savings account, certificate of deposit, life insurance policy (assuming this policy meets the definition of a life insurance policy and is not an investment account in disguise) or commercial annuity does not meet the definition of a passive foreign investment company.[15]

---

[15] For more information contact your tax advisor or visit: http://www.irs.gov/instructions/i8621/index.html. For a copy of Form 8621 visit: http://www.irs.gov/pub/irs-pdf/f8621.pdf

Finally, new rules generally require annual reporting of PFICs. Don't panic if you own them, some planning may go a long way here. At the same time, before you make any investment decisions, you should make sure you know exactly what you're getting into.

Estate and Gift Taxation

U.S Citizens and U.S.-domiciled Foreign Citizens

For U.S. citizens and individuals "domiciled" in the United States, the gift and estate taxes are coordinated in one unified system. We have covered the concept of domicile, but to briefly summarize, a non-U.S. person may considered to be domiciled in the United States if they reside in the United States and intend to remain there indefinitely. It is also possible for a non-U.S. person, non-resident of the United States, to be domiciled in the United States if there is intention to return to the United States and consider it to be their permanent home. Permanent residents (aka green card holders) will likely be considered domiciled in the United States.

The United States estate and gift tax rules apply to assets and gifts worldwide. A U.S. citizen or domiciliary is allowed to give up to USD 14,000 per year (2017) free of tax for each separate person to whom you give gifts. The 2018 amount is USD 15,000. If you are gifting to a spouse who is a U.S. citizen, you are allowed unlimited gifts. Otherwise, the gift to your spouse is limited to USD 149,000 in 2017 (USD 152,000 in 2018).

When you make any gifts in excess of these annual limits, you have made "taxable gifts," and these gifts must be reported and tracked on an annual gift tax return. When your cumulative taxable gifts exceed a lifetime maximum of USD 5,490,000 in 2017, the excess is subject to gift tax at a maximum rate of forty percent. The 2017 Tax

Act[16] (formerly known as the *Tax Cuts and Jobs Act of 2017*) doubled the base estate and gift tax exemption amount for the period after December 31, 2017 and before January 1, 2026. This results in the 2018 figure to be approximately USD 11,200,000 (USD 22,400,000 per married couple).

At death, the estate tax may apply. The taxable value of the estate is the value of all assets at the date of death, reduced by transfers to your U.S. citizen spouse, bequests to U.S. charitable organizations and liabilities. It is further reduced by any portion of the lifetime exclusion that has not already been used against taxable gifts, the remainder is taxed at a maximum rate in the same way described for gifts above.

Non-domiciled, Non-U.S. Person

On November 11, 1988, President Ronald Reagan, in his last major formal announcement, signed the Technical and Miscellaneous Revenue Act (TAMRA) of 1988, making adjustments to the Tax Reform Act of 1986. There are two major provisions in TAMRA that affect foreign owners of U.S. property.

The first provision is a dramatic increase in estate or death taxes for non-residents on their U.S. property. The applicable Treasury Regulations contain specific rules for determining the situs of particular types of assets. For example, real property (e.g. fixed property, principally land and buildings compared to personal property) located in the United States is considered a United States situs asset as is stock issued by a corporation organized in the United States, whereas the stock of a foreign corporation is considered a foreign situs asset. The value of the non-resident, non-U.S. citizen taxable estate in excess of USD 60,000 is taxed at a maximum rate of

---

[16] On December 20, the House approved H.R. 1, the "Tax Cuts and Jobs Act" however due to the fact that the bill was moved under "budget reconciliation" the official title of the final bill became "An Act to provide for reconciliation pursuant to titles II and V of the concurrent resolution on the budget for fiscal year 2018". I use 2017 Tax Act to represent this title.

40%. As referenced earlier, the United States has special estate tax treaties with certain countries.

Here is an example of how a non-U.S. family may be affected by these rules:

Charles is an executive in an overseas office of a U.S. company. He participates in the employee benefit package offered by the company, which includes the issuance of company stock and stock options. The shares are held in Charles' U.S. brokerage account, which he was encouraged to open by the plan administrator. Charles is not a U.S. citizen. He currently resides outside of the United States and he has never lived in the U.S.

Charles is newly married, to a non-U.S. citizen. Together, Charles and his wife have twin two-year-old boys.

Charles is revisiting his retirement and legacy goals with us. He understands that the dividends paid on the stock are subject to income tax of 30%, withheld at source, and also that he is not subject to capital gains tax on the sale of the stock as long as he does not trigger U.S. residency or obtain U.S. citizenship. No income or estate tax treaty is in place between the United States and Charles' home country, where he is also a resident.

Although the value of assets appeared to fund the financial independence goal, substantial risk to the actual achievement of this goal exists in the form of a U.S. estate tax liability. If Charles were to die today, his young family would face a large U.S. tax liability that would be payable nine months after the date of his death.

Gift and estate tax free transfers from a non-domiciled, non-U.S. person to a U.S. citizen spouse are unlimited. As mentioned earlier, reporting may be required.

Wealth Transfer to a Non-U.S. Citizen Spouse

The second provision of TAMRA is the loss of the marital deduction in the case where the surviving spouse is not a citizen of the Unites States.

The rationale for this treatment was that such a spouse would be free to leave the United States and take any inherited assets out of the U.S. This would have the effect of transforming what had been intended as a mere "deferral" of the married couples' full estate tax (e.g., by waiting until the death of the survivor to impose the full estate tax) into an "escape" from the estate tax entirely. This is because if the surviving spouse were not a U.S. citizen it would be fairly easy (and perhaps not unlikely) to leave the United States, with inherited assets. In that case, none of the three jurisdictional bases (citizenship, domicile, or location of assets) would apply.

To prevent this potential "escape" the new rules required that if the marital deduction were to be allowed it would be only with respect to assets that were transferred to a new entity, a "Qualified Domestic Trust" (QDOT). There are a number of rules associated with a QDOT, which should be considered with counsel.

13

EMPLOYEE BENEFITS AND RETIREMENT PLANS

Whether you work for yourself or someone else, you'll need to have an understanding of the different compensation-related benefits that your *Cross-Border Life + Wealth Achievement Plan* will need to consider. These will generally include compensatory benefits such as retirement plans, deferred compensation and stock options, and/or share grants.

Deferred Compensation

Deferred Compensation is compensation that you earn in one year but do not receive until a later year. The general idea is that if the employer meets certain conditions regarding how it's paid, deferred compensation is not taxable until the compensation is received. However, avoiding tax in the year the compensation is earned cannot be achieved simply by asking an employer to defer payment. The employer must set up a deferred compensation plan that meets complex rules to obtain U.S. tax deferral.

Making non-U.S. based deferred compensation arrangements conform with U.S. rules can be complex, so the acceptance of these benefits should be subject to a review of how they may impact you.

Some non-qualified deferred compensation plans can require that you pay tax on the deferred amount in the year it is earned rather than the year it is received. An additional 20% tax may also be assessed on the deferred income. Most foreign retirement plans will look like non-qualified deferred compensation plans, with the specific treatment being subject to various rules which we'll look at a little closer later in this section.

A common misconception is that funds from a foreign pension plan may be rolled over into a U.S. qualified retirement plan such as a 401k, IRA, or Roth IRA account. However, this is never possible with any type of foreign retirement account because they are rarely, if ever, going to meet the Internal Revenue Code requirements so that they are considered a U.S. qualified plan. If the plan does not meet the U.S. qualified plan rules, then proceeds from the plan cannot roll into a U.S. qualified plan. A much more common scenario is that the foreign country will allow you to withdraw funds when you permanently leave the country or convert the plan to an immediate annuity or some other form of distribution when you meet the eligibility for withdrawal, normally at retirement age. When and how you are able to withdraw funds from a local plan is country specific and dual nationals will potentially be caught between rules covering local citizens and guest workers if their home country only allows withdrawal on leaving the country for guest workers.

Employer Stock

For many global executives and managers of international companies, the value of employer shares and options account for a large percentage of their contingent assets (aside from their human capital, of course). As is the case with any concentrated position, the risks to the *Cross Border Life + Wealth Achievement Plan* can be high, depending on various circumstances.

Stock Options and Share Grants

Employers often grant shares and stock options as compensation. A stock option is the right to purchase shares in a corporation at a price that is fixed when the option is issued. The option agreement usually specifies the purchase price and time period during which the option can be exercised. For U.S. tax purposes, how the exercise of a stock option is taxed depends on whether it's an "incentive stock option (ISO)" or a "non-qualified option."

An ISO is an option that meets certain U.S. requirements regarding its price, when it can be exercised and how many options can be exercised. Your employer will have structured the award so that the option qualifies for ISO treatment. If you hold the stock for at least two years from the date of the grant of the option and one year from the date you exercise the option, you will not be taxed on the grant or exercise of an ISO. In addition, if you meet these time requirements, you will be taxed at the capital gains tax rates when you sell the stock (which is not the typical taxation of compensation). On the other hand, if you sell the stock too soon and thus do not meet the time requirements, the difference between the fair market value of the stock at the time of exercise and the amount you paid at exercise is taxed as compensation at ordinary rates. Although there is no regular income tax assessed at the time of grant or exercise of an ISO, the excess of the fair market value of the stock at the date of exercise over the purchase price is added back as an adjustment to taxable income for alternative minimum tax (AMT) purposes.

A non-qualified stock option is any option, other than an ISO, that is granted as compensation for services. In most cases, you won't be subject to tax on the grant of a non-qualified stock option. When you exercise a non-qualified stock option you are taxed on the fair market value of the stock received, less its purchase price. The subsequent sale of the stock will result in a capital gain or loss. In determining gain or loss, the basis of the stock is the purchase price plus the compensation recognized at exercise. Unlike the ISO, there is no adjustment for alternative minimum tax purposes at exercise.

Cross-Border Stock Option Tax Planning Issues

Holders of employer stock-options and share grants who perform services or reside in different countries during the term of the grants face the risk of double taxation.

Benefits arising from this type of compensation can be broken down into three separate events:

1. *Time of grant (or when it vests).* Usually, the option is granted free of charge or below market value at the time of grant.

2. *Exercise of option.* A share of employer stock is acquired, usually at a price below market value. The benefit, which is usually taxed, corresponds to the difference between the price paid and the market value of the share at the time.[17]

3. *Sale of shares.* Shares owned as a result of exercise may be sold at any time in the future, realizing a gain to the extent that the share value has increased since the exercise date.

The table below provides one example of how these events might come into being. For the sake of simplicity, the chart shows the grant of a share option in year one, vesting after two years in year three, followed by exercise of the option in year four and subsequent sale in year five.

---

[17] Another benefit that may arise is that of dividend income, if the employer stock pays dividends, and assuming the shares are not immediately sold. Consideration of this fact should be included in one's analysis of the benefits.

Year	1	2	3	4	5
Event	Grant or sale of share option		End of vesting period and acquisition of share	Exercise of option	Sale of shares
Price	Price of option		Market price of share acquired	Strike price	Market price of share sold
Value	Value of option at grant		Value of option at end vesting period	Value of option at exercise. Value of share acquired	Value of share sold

I have also included the events that may require valuation. Valuation is another issue to be considered during the planning process. Valuation may be complicated due to currency exchange issues and the formula used to determine value.

A change in residence during the timeframe between events and the fact that the benefits from an employee stock option may taxed at different times in different countries is a significant financial planning challenge.

A country may tax the benefits resulting from an employee stock option at one or more of the following events:

- At the time the option is granted.

- At the time of vesting.

- At the time an employee ceases residency.

- When the option is exercised.

- When there are no longer any restrictions on the sale of the shares; or

- When the shares are sold.[18]

The example below illustrates the situation where taxation may occur at different times in different countries:

Tom, who is a resident of Country A, worked six months in Country B. Part of his remuneration from employment in Country B were stock options of XYZ Company, a resident of Country B. According to the laws of Country B, the employment benefit resulting from the stock options is taxed when the shares are sold and is deemed to correspond to the difference between the sale price of the shares and the strike price paid by the employee.

In Country A, the employment benefit arising from stock options corresponds to the difference between the value of the shares when the option was exercised and the amount paid by the employee; that benefit is taxed when the option is exercised. So, assuming Tom exercises the option in year one, he will be taxed in Country A. He sells the shares in year three, when Country B taxes him on the gain.

Additional complications arise if an individual resides in different countries at the time an option is granted, the time it vests and the shares are sold. In addition, the risk of taxation as a result of multiple residences could be compounded in the case of countries that deem capital gains to be realized when a person ceases residency or that maintain, through their tax conventions a right to tax capital gains of former residents.

---

[18] Depending on the countries involved, the tax treatment of the benefits arising from a stock option or the resulting gain from the sale of shares may differ depending on how long the shares have been owned after their acquisition by the employee.

Income tax treaties typically resolve the problem of double taxation in three ways. First, conflicts arising from the mutual exertion of residence basis taxation are resolved by assigning the individual only one country of tax residence. If an individual meets the residency test of both countries then the treaty tiebreaker provisions apply to determine only one tax residence for treaty purposes.[19] Second, various categories of income, (e.g. investment income and wages), are assigned a source and the jurisdiction to tax is allocated between the source and residence country. Finally, for income property subject to both residence and source basis taxation, in the relief-from-double-taxation article, treaties provide that the residence country must cede its jurisdiction to tax, to the source country by either granting a credit for source basis taxes or exempting source country income.[20]

As seen by the examples above, when different countries tax the same income at different periods and the individual is subject to residence basis taxation for each period; however, treaties do not resolve these conflicts in a way that prevents double taxation.

Restricted Stock Units

Restricted stock units (RSU) are a way your employer can grant company shares to you as an employee. The grant is "restricted" because it's subject to a vesting schedule, which can be based on length of employment or on performance goals, and because it is governed by other limits on transfers or sales that your company can impose. Unlike stock options, which can go "underwater" and lose all practical value with a falling stock price, RSUs are almost always worth something, even if the stock price drops dramatically.

---

[19] See OECD Model Treaty *supra* note 15, at art. 4
[20] Ibid. at art. 23A, 23B.

With RSUs, you are taxed when the shares are received, which is almost always at vesting. Your taxable income is the market value of the shares at vesting, taxed as compensation. When you sell the shares, you will pay capital gains tax on any appreciation over the market price of the shares on the vesting date. It's possible that you may receive dividend income from shares that are not yet vested. In this case, the income will be treated as compensation.

The 2017 Tax Act (H.R. 1) and Qualified Equity Grant Deferral

The 2017 Tax Act (formerly and more commonly known as the "Tax Cuts and Jobs Act") added Section 83(i) to the Internal Revenue Code. Generally this provides an opportunity for non-executive and non-highly compensated employees of a privately held corporation to elect up to a five-year deferral in the taxation of illiquid shares issued to them upon the exercise of nonqualified options or the settlement of restricted stock units (RSU) so long as certain conditions are satisfied. Many restrictions apply therefore this type of plan may not become widely used; however, I include it here to reduce confusion and raise awareness.

Retirement Plans

Tax policy in many countries provides incentives designed to encourage employers to establish and fund retirement plans for their workers. In certain countries, favorable tax treatment is tied to requirements regarding eligibility and coverage that are designed to ensure that a pension plan benefits a cross-section of workers. However, these incentives may not carry over to guest workers.

Whether you are a U.S. citizen or resident or a foreign national resident for income tax purposes in the United States, you will want to understand how your planning is affected by the way the United States views retirement plans.

It bears repeating here that we are primarily looking at rules from a United States point of view in this part of the book. When it comes to taxation, *remember that residency matters* and therefore *if and when* you are resident in another country, the rules of that country will also need to be taken into consideration. Bi-lateral tax treaties may provide some guidance.

Qualified Plans

In the United States, employer-sponsored plans that meet the legal requirements are referred to as qualified plans. A plan participant, who moves from one country to another but remains with the same employer may, depending on the length of foreign assignment, be permitted to accrue service credits and/or continue to make contributions into the same pension plan that provided coverage before the transfer. In this situation, the internationally mobile employee may not see his or her retirement savings affected by an international posting, and in conjunction with the assignment, an employee transferred by an employer may receive tax advice and perhaps even tax equalization payments from the employer to counteract any additional tax that accrues.

Retirement plan distribution income received from U.S. or non-U.S. plans are generally taxable when received. If you did not contribute to the cost of the pension amount being distributed, the full amount received is generally taxable. If you did contribute, a portion of pension amounts received may be excluded from your gross income. The rules for determining the non-taxable portion can be complicated, particularly when the distribution is from a non-U.S. plan. Therefore, it is extremely important for non-U.S. pension plans that you retain documentation to support and potentially to calculate this amount.

The typical qualified plans include an employer or individual 401(k) plan, 403(b) plan or possibly a defined benefit plan. Other qualified plans include the traditional Individual Retirement Plan (IRA) and the Roth IRA or Roth 401(k).

Traditional 401(k) Plan

A 401(k) is an employer-sponsored retirement plan that allows tax-deferred contributions to be made. For 2017 you may contribute up to USD 18,000 (or USD 24,000 if age 50 or older). Employer contributions typically come in the form of matching contributions, where an employer agrees to supplement your contributions up to a certain amount; however, some employers make profit-sharing contributions that aren't connected to how much an employee contributes.

The combined total of annual contributions to all of your defined contribution plan accounts—this includes elective deferrals, employee contributions, employer matching and discretionary contributions and allocations of forfeitures to your accounts—may not exceed the lesser of 100% of your compensation or USD 54,000 for 2017 (USD 60,000 if 50 or over). In addition, the amount of your compensation that can be taken into account when determining employer and employee contributions is limited. The compensation limitation is USD 270,000 in 2017 (USD 265,000 in 2016).

If plans do not meet certain requirements, the rules that affect Highly Compensated Employees (earnings of more than USD 120,000) can reduce the amount of allowed contributions.

Individual Retirement Account (IRA)

An Individual Retirement Account allows a U.S. person to contribute up to USD 5,500 (or USD 6,500 if over age 50) in 2017, if you have Modified Adjusted Gross Income (e.g. earned income that has not been excluded by the FEIE and the Foreign Housing Cost Exclusions) of at least this amount. Investments in and IRA account grow tax-deferred until withdrawal. At age 59 ½ distributions can begin. Starting at age 70 ½ minimum annual distributions based on your life expectancy become mandatory. Distributions are typically fully taxable at ordinary income rates. In addition to annual contributions, you may also fund a traditional IRA account through a tax-free transfer from another qualified plan.

Generally, the amount contributed to an IRA can be taken as a deduction against gross income, but this benefit is phased out at higher income levels, although you are still permitted to make non-deductible contributions.

If you are covered by a qualified employer-sponsored retirement plan your eligibility to contribute pre-tax dollars to an IRA may be partially or completely eliminated.

Roth IRA

You can contribute the same amount to a Roth IRA that you can to a traditional IRA; however, contributions to both kinds of IRAs in a given year cannot when combined exceed the USD 5,500 limitation (USD 6,500 if age 50 or older). Contributions to Roth IRAs are never tax deductible, but earnings inside the plan grow tax-free and withdrawals from this plan upon reaching retirement age are not subject to income tax.

Eligibility to make contributions to a Roth IRA is limited based on modified adjusted gross income (MAGI). As described earlier, that is AGI unreduced by the foreign earned income exclusion and foreign housing cost exclusion. Here is the chart for 2017.

2017 MAGI Limits for Roth IRA contributions		
If your filing status is…	And your modified AGI is…	Then you can contribute…
single, head of household or married filing separately and you did not live with your spouse at any time during the year	< USD118,000	Up to the limit (USD 5,500/6,500)
	≥ USD118,000 but < USD 133,000	A reduced amount
	≥ USD133,000	zero
married filing separately and you lived with your spouse at any time during the year	< USD10,000	A reduced amount
	≥ USD10,000	zero
married filing jointly or qualifying widow(er)	< USD184,000	Up to the limit
	≥ USD184,000 but < USD 194,000	A reduced amount
	≥ USD194,000	zero

The chart above shows that single filers or those with head of household filing status with modified adjusted gross income above USD 133,000 and married, filing jointly filers with modified adjusted gross income above the amount of USD 194,000 cannot contribute to a Roth IRA. In addition, if your filing status is married filing separate (as is often the situation where U.S. persons are married to non-U.S.

persons and live outside the United States), you cannot contribute to a Roth IRA if your modified adjusted gross income is USD 10,000 or above.

The advisability of a Roth IRA requires a complex evaluation of where you expect to be resident and the tax environment you will be in at the time of payout versus your situation at the time you are eligible to make a contribution. In addition, although the grow inside the plan is tax free by the United States, it is possible that a country in which you are resident may wish to tax that growth. Tax credits or a treaty may be available, and that information would need to be factored into the analysis.

The opportunity to convert an existing IRA into a Roth account requires a similar analysis.

Non-qualified Plans

If you are self-employed or if you move from one country to another while also changing employers, you will need to deal with the intricacies of provisions regarding individual taxation of plan distributions and provisions for individual retirement savings as detailed in the following section.

While foreign pensions are a very common feature of living outside the United States, they involve a number of complex U.S. tax considerations that can vary significantly from plan to plan. For this reason, foreign pension plans are one of the most misunderstood and mishandled items on the U.S. federal income tax return.

Reporting a foreign pension plan or any other deferred compensation plan properly on a U.S. tax return is a time consuming, and therefore typically expensive, task. Financial interest in each of the plans or accounts will form part of your foreign reporting (Form 8938 and FBAR), and possibly Form 3520 relating to U.S. owners of foreign trusts. If the pension plan does not meet certain requirements, Form 8621 reporting for Passive Foreign Investment Companies (PFIC) may also need to be filed to report underlying investments. Proper compliance is complicated by the lack of information from the foreign pension plan sponsor and uncertainty regarding the best reporting methods among tax preparers.

While foreign pension plans can take a variety of different forms, a typical overseas plan involves a private arrangement that provides for the provision of retirement benefits in connection with employment and allows for the deferral of taxation on plan contributions and earnings in the country where the plan is established. In this sense, foreign pension plans can be distinguished from social security arrangements, which are government-managed income subsidy systems funded by taxpayers.

An important starting point in analyzing the taxation of a foreign pension plan is determining whether the plan should be classified as a trust for U.S. federal income tax purposes. This is because Section 402(b) of the Code provides helpful rules for employees' trusts that do not qualify for full U.S. tax deferral. In this regard, the IRS has ruled in a number of instances that particular foreign pension plans (including so-called "superannuation funds") should be treated as trusts for U.S. tax purposes.

Assuming trust classification, the taxation of employer contributions and earnings will then depend on whether the foreign pension plan is "discriminatory" or not. This is determined based on the plan coverage ratio of highly compensated employees to non-highly compensated employees. Highly compensated employees are defined to include those with certain employer ownership interests or employees that have an annual compensation above a certain level.

As a general rule, under Section 402(b), in the case of non-discriminatory pension plans, employees must currently include employer contributions in income but can defer tax on pension earnings until withdrawal upon retirement. In the case of discriminatory plans, the highly compensated employees may need to currently include both contributions and earnings in income. On the upside, paying tax currently generally means that you will not have to pay tax on a future withdrawal upon retirement due to the tax basis that is being built inside the plan. Note: You will need to ensure that you track your tax basis otherwise you will pay tax twice: First at the time of receipt to you as compensation income and then again as income on distribution.

A number of additional factors further complicate the situation, including whether your interest in a pension plan is considered "vested" for tax purposes, and whether the pension plan is actually funded with employer and/or employee contributions. On top of all this, the general U.S. tax treatment of a pension plan may be overridden by the provisions of a relevant tax treaty that contains a pension provision.

In the case of foreign pension plans that qualify as employees' trusts, Forms 3520 and 3520-A, which deal with foreign trust reporting, may be triggered if your contributions to the plan exceed that of your employer. In such case, the employee is considered the owner of the employee contribution portion of the trust under the "grantor" trust rules, and the trust is bifurcated into two pieces. The piece qualifying as a grantor trust has a filing requirement on Forms 3520 and 3520-A and may have additional reporting requirements depending on the pension's underlying investments (e.g., PFIC reporting). If the employer contributions exceed the employee contributions, the entire plan is generally treated as a "non-grantor" trust that does not trigger a 3520 or 3520-A filing obligation.

Foreign Individual Retirement Savings Plans

Foreign individual retirement plans may be created from a rollover of money from a foreign employer-sponsored plan or simply funded as a savings plan. These plans will have any number of names and may be "locked-in" until retirement in keeping with the laws of the country in which it is located. Some plans that are actually treated as foreign grantor trusts for U.S. tax and reporting purposes may appear to be an insurance product on first glance.

These plans are generally considered grantor trusts by the United States, with the treatment being as described for the employee portion of an employer-sponsored plan that is determined to be bifurcated. Foreign individual retirement savings accounts may be limited to investing in PFICs. This causes the complex intersection of trust reporting with PFIC reporting.

Given the potential tax exposure and large penalties, it is important to understand the tax treatment of these pension plans and their tax reporting requirements, as well as their underlying investment options and the fees associated with them, and plan accordingly.

Social Security Benefits Across Borders

Social Security (also known as Old Age Pension) is another area in cross-border planning that causes a lot of confusion.

Each country has its own program, with its own rules and formulas for contributions and benefits. Most of the time contributions made while living and working in a given country will not have reached the level required to receive full benefits. Therefore, it's common without any planning for someone to potentially receive partial benefits in a variety of countries, in various currencies.

The United States has bilateral agreements with twenty-six countries that exist to coordinate the U.S. Social Security program with the comparable program of the other country. International Social Insurance agreements, typically called "Totalization agreements," exist to eliminate double taxation on the same earnings.

These agreements also help to fill in gaps in benefit protection. Workers who have divided their careers between the United States and a foreign country sometimes fail to qualify for retirement, survivors or disability insurance benefits (pensions) from one or both countries because they have not worked long enough or recently enough to meet minimum eligibility requirements. Under an agreement, such workers may qualify for partial U.S. or foreign benefits based on combined, or "totalized" coverage credits from both countries.

Dual Social Security tax liability is a common challenge for people working for U.S. multinational companies because the U.S. Social Security program covers U.S. citizens and U.S. residents employed outside the United States, even if hired abroad. This affects multinationals and foreign affiliates of an American company, if the U.S. company has entered into an agreement with the Department of Treasury to provide Social Security coverage for U.S. citizens and residents employed by the affiliate.

Paying dual Social Security contributions is particularly costly for companies that offer "tax equalization" arrangements. Under this arrangement, the employer will typically agree to pay both the employer and employee share of the foreign or "host" country Social Security taxes on behalf of their transferred employee. However, the tax laws of many countries will consider the employer payment of an employee's share of a Social Security contribution to be taxable compensation to the employee, thus increasing the employee's income tax liability. The tax equalization arrangement generally provides that the employer will also pay this additional income tax, which only serves to increase the employee's taxable income and tax liability even further. The employer again pays the additional tax and the circle continues.

For countries where these bilateral agreements exist, it is important to become familiar with the coverage and exemptions.

Certificates of Coverage

If you are exempt from U.S. or foreign Social Security taxes under an agreement, you must document your exemption by obtaining a certificate of coverage from the country that will continue to cover you.

For example, if you are sent on temporary assignment to the United Kingdom, you would need a certificate of coverage issued by the Social Security Administration to prove your exemption from U.K. Social Insurance contributions. Conversely, if you are a U.K.-based employee working temporarily in the United States, you would need a certificate from the U.K. authorities as evidence of the exemption from U.S. Social Security tax.

Generally, when the Social Security Administration issues a certificate certifying U.S. coverage, a copy of the certificate usually must be presented to the appropriate foreign authorities as proof of entitlement to the foreign exemption. When the other country issues a certificate certifying that you are covered by the foreign system, your employer can immediately stop withholding and paying U.S. Social Security taxes on your earnings. The certificate should just be retained so that it can be produced in the event the Internal Revenue Service ever questions why no taxes are being paid. If you are a self-employed U.S. citizen or resident, you must attach a photocopy of the foreign certificate to your U.S. tax return each year as proof of the

U.S. exemption from self-employment taxes for the period shown on the certificate.

For a list of countries and details of agreement coverage and benefits, visit https://www.ssa.gov/international/agreement_descriptions.html.

U.S. Social Security Payments Outside the United States

Generally, the benefits you earn won't be lost if you are not living in the United States at the time you wish to receive payments. However, some restrictions apply to *where* payments can be made.

Possible Reduction of Benefits

A common challenge for U.S. citizens and residents is the Windfall Elimination Provision (WEP). This provision primarily affects you if you worked in the United States long enough to qualify for a Social Security retirement benefit and also earned a public pension benefit from a foreign country based on contributions paid in while working in that foreign country and on which U.S. Social Security taxes were not paid.

For people in this situation who reach 62 or became disabled in or after 1990, the formula used to calculate your full Primary Insurance Amount (PIA) is adjusted depending on the number of years of substantial earnings on which Social Security taxes were paid.

Online calculators and additional details can be obtained directly from the Social Security Administration website.[21]

---

[21] https://www.ssa.gov/international/

14

WEALTH TRANSFER AND LEGACY

A family moves from rags, to riches, to rags, in three generations
—Proverb

In this chapter, we'll explore a number of extremely critical non-tax issues that must be considered whenever more than one country is involved in the wealth transfer planning for an individual or family.

Family Legal Definitions

There are a variety of issues that can be involved with respect to the legal family relationships. These would include the following questions:

1.   Would the spouse be recognized as such?

2.   Was there a prior divorce that would not be recognized?

3.   Would a "common law" spouse be recognized?

4.   Would a "same sex" spouse be recognized?

5.   Will an adopted child be recognized?

Override by Family Protection Acts

There are an increasing number of jurisdictions that have passed legislation under which a challenge may be made against a Will that someone was not treated "fairly." Usually entitled some form of "family protection act" these can be used to override the terms of a Will.

Marital Property Regimes

Generally, a marital property regime determines how assets acquired prior to, and during, a marriage are distributed.

Community property is a marital property regime that originated in civil law jurisdictions, and is now also found in some common law jurisdictions. In a community property jurisdiction, most property acquired during the marriage (except for gifts or inheritances) is owned jointly by both spouses and is divided upon divorce, annulment, or death.

As an initial matter, one needs to consider whether or not a married person, particularly one from another jurisdiction, in fact has the legal right to control the inheritance of all of his or her property. This is another area that can be extremely complex.

If there is a "marital property" regime the spouse may normally dispose of only his or her separate property interest. Those regimes vary considerably and it's not always easy to determine which regime will apply. There may also be forced heirship rights, which could result in there being only a small percentage of property that one might dispose of by a will.

Forced Heirship

In civil law jurisdictions there are also rules about the rights of children to inherit a fixed portion of a parent's estate. A planning opportunity exists, as the enforcement of these rights may depend upon the forum in which a particular issue is presented.

The manner in which forced heirship rules operate can vary considerably by country. The amounts can differ, the lifetime freedom of disposition by gift may have differing restrictions, and in some cases amounts that have been given away during lifetime can be "clawed back" into the estate. As with other issues of this nature, a knowledgeable practitioner in the other country should be consulted.

Lack of Probate

In civil law jurisdictions the concept of "probate" is not a familiar one. There is instead an "immediate" inheritance by the heirs of the assets, as well as the liabilities (unless a procedure is used to examine the assets and liabilities first).

Non-recognition of Trusts

Many countries of the world, most notably those countries based in civil law (which includes the countries of Western Europe) do not recognize the legal concept of a trust (with the exception of the few that have adopted the Hague Convention on the Recognition of Trusts).

The intersection of foreign and domestic law extends beyond the tax consequences of transactions and mobility. Tax consequences attach to different types of taxpayers. For example, the tax consequences may differ if income is earned by an individual, a trust, a partnership or a corporation. Therefore, your cross-border planner and team may be required to determine, in certain situations, whether an entity is a trust, a partnership, a corporation, or something else.

The problem of determining tax consequences on the basis of the underlying legal situation is exacerbated in the cross-border context because the domestic tax consequences often must be determined on the basis of the legal concepts of the foreign country.

Selecting the Most Appropriate Entity

Selecting the most effective type of entity to use when developing a cross-border financial plan is an essential part of accomplishing your goals. This task is made more complex by the differences in language and legal systems around the world. Entities such as trusts, limited liability companies, partnerships and corporations, although used extensively in North America, are not treated uniformly or recognized around the world.

Business organizations like the Limited Liability Company (LLC) have added financial planning opportunities by offering the company advantages of limited liability and centralized management. However, an LLC may be characterized as tax transparent by one jurisdiction with which it has some economic or legal connection, but as non-transparent by another jurisdiction.

For example, a holding company incorporated as an LLC seeks to invest in publicly traded companies of Country A. The LLC is incorporated and owned by people of Country B. The laws of Country A define the entity as a flow-through entity for income tax purposes, whereas in Country B, there is no flow-through treatment.

The concept of a partnership and the concept of a trust both may have different meanings in different countries. Due to the complexities involved in both these situations and individual circumstances and goals, structuring is an advanced concept beyond the scope of this book.

"Situs" versus Multiple Wills

A mention of "death" brings an interesting pause to any social gathering, and discussing wills has about the same effect on most people. *I should get around to making a will* passes fleetingly through the minds of most people at some stage in their lives. However, the truth is that the majority never does, and the perceived wisdom appears to be that people would rather trust the government to distribute their estate, than spend a short amount of time making their own arrangements. Additionally, the threat to expatriate workers' lives is greater than ever before — and there can be serious implications for both employers and families if an expatriate worker dies while on assignment.

The subject of an expatriate's death while on assignment has generally been an unmentionable subject, dealt with by employers on a case-by-case basis. But, with an escalation in threats to expat's lives from, for instance, terrorism, kidnapping, natural disasters, civil unrest and disease, more systematic planning has become essential.

Administrative Matters of Death Abroad

The common perception of what happens when a loved one dies is that the funeral has to be arranged and legal counsel must be contacted to distribute the estate. While these are certainly two of the tasks that must be undertaken, they are by no means the *only* two. The death and ensuing responsibilities are difficult and stressful enough for those living at home, but would you know what to do if your partner died while you were living outside of your passport country?

In the unfortunate event of the death outside of your passport country, the death may be registered at the local embassy of the person's birth country. The details of the death will be entered in a death register, and a death certificate will be issued.

Generally, if the next-of-kin wishes for the remains to be repatriated to the birth country for burial or cremation, the death usually must be registered with the Embassy. To apply for the death to be registered, the local death certificate and the deceased's original passport must be produced.

If the deceased has a will, ensure you know with which law firm it is held, or if the deceased kept the will themselves, ensure you take it back to your home country with you. Upon repatriation, contact the law firm who holds the will or approach legal counsel near you — ideally one who knows the family and knew the deceased.

Wills and Probate Across Jurisdictions

Unless you make a will, you cannot guarantee that your belongings, when you die, will be distributed as you wish. Many unnecessary complications arise, adding to the grief of family and friends, and the expense of winding up the estate. If you die without a will (intestate) the law provides who will receive your possessions.

If you are married, but die intestate, it is a common misconception that your surviving spouse inherits everything. This is usually not the case, and depends on the size of the estate, and whom you leave behind and the jurisdictions involved. Often, if you are not married but living with your partner and die intestate, your partner will receive nothing. Leaving things to chance is not only a selfish act, it can be a certain way of ensuring that large sums of money are wasted on legal and court fees, while gifting tax authorities a large proportion of everything you worked to accumulate in your lifetime.

Similarly, because the rules keep changing (as do individual circumstances), it is essential to review the plans that you made, to make sure that what you thought was going to happen with your money is what is *actually* going to happen. The process can be as simple or as complex as you wish to make it, but the requirement must be that you should do something.

While it may not be paramount to write a will in every country where you hold property, if you do so, it will make the job for your executors a great deal simpler if they are given the power to implement and enforce your wishes in each jurisdiction.

One of the main problems that can arise is the treatment of the expatriate's estate by the host jurisdiction. A will, prepared under the laws of the expatriate's home country, at worst, might be completely invalid under the laws in the host country. Even if the host country recognizes the will, certain aspects of it might be unenforceable.

This could cause tremendous financial and other strain to surviving family members, and could lead to the family incurring substantial legal costs in trying to sort out the situation.

Closely tied to the issue of wills and estate planning is the possibility of unanticipated additional taxes. Many countries, especially in the developed world, impose "death taxes" in a variety of forms — some on the estate of the deceased, and others on the beneficiaries of the estate of the deceased. Careful planning can often greatly reduce these taxes.

While many countries have tax treaties to avoid double taxation, an existing treaty does not necessarily mean it will be easy to determine which of the two jurisdictions (or more, depending on asset location) has primary taxing rights. The situation is often complicated by the location of assets, the citizenship of the deceased, and where the deceased was actually domiciled or resident at the time of death.

If you are overseas due to an employment situation, check with your employer as to what is covered in your employer's expatriate tax policy. If "death taxes" are not covered, you're responsible for making sure your family and beneficiaries are protected from additional taxation.

Enduring Powers of Attorney and Living Wills

Many documents drafted in one jurisdiction for use will not be recognized or given effect in other jurisdictions.

Writing Your Chapter of the Family History

The lifestyle of transnational and multinational families causes, for the most part, a dislocation of the "traditional" extended family. For many it means that grandparents, grandchildren — and increasingly great-grandparents and great-grandchildren — are separated by bodies of water or geographic distance. The ethical will, tantamount to the family mission statement, is a way to have continuity when we don't live with, or close to one another. It's a way to express intangible characteristics, experiences and belief that constitute the personal and social dimensions of your life map. It can also link the past to the present.

An *ethical will* is an ancient Hebraic tradition of passing on the substance of their emotional life, including their accomplishments, fears, aspirations, lessons learned and hopes for the future. It originates in the religions of the West. In their simplest form, ethical wills are letters, usually addressed to grown children, recounting family history and expressing hope that the writer will be remembered for certain values. At their most urgent, they are letters that begin, "If I don't make it home, I want you to know…"

An ethical will is not intended to replace a traditional will or to address the division of one's property. It is more about what you want your loved ones to know or have in a *figurative* sense, than about what you want them to inherit in a *literal* sense. Many people choosing to craft ethical wills, also known as personal legacy statements, have embraced the practice as a chance to do more than communicate practical information. Many are choosing ethical wills or personal legacy statements as a way of imparting some of their wisdom and experiences to their loved ones — as a way of telling their stories.

The ethical will discuss the values, experiences and beliefs that have shaped the author, the values they wish to pass along to descendants, and what their hopes are for future generations. In an age when families are spread across the world and in which a second or third generation of family members may have had few opportunities to interact with the founding donor, having a written statement of values can provide much-needed guidance during times of decision. Having this sort of document also increase the chances that geographically separated family members, collaborating on their philanthropy from afar, will share an understanding of the goals they are striving for.

Keep in mind though, that the world in which you founded your philanthropy is not necessarily the world in which it will always operate. In fact, as philanthropists, we hope that it won't be — that some social ills will be cured by our work and the work of grantees, and that positive change is occurring. By leaving behind a personal legacy statement and ensuring your successors are aware of what has been important to you and your family, they will be better equipped to make decisions that could fulfill your philanthropy's goals. The purpose of drafting an ethical will or donor legacy statement is not to bind your family to the past in a way that is restrictive or cumbersome, but rather to add to your collective family history and to enable them to write their own chapters.

How Do I Get Started?

For starters, consider what about the idea of an ethical will or personal legacy statement appeals to you and what you hope to accomplish by completing one. These goals might include:

- To supplement or personalize the terms of your existing, traditional will.

- To share your hopes for the future of your family and its philanthropy.

- To reach out to loved ones with whom you have lost touch or who have been separated by geographic distance.

- To document your family's history or your own life experiences.

- To reaffirm the relationships with those closest to you.

Next, you may wish to begin keeping a journal or diary as a collecting point for your ideas. Typically, authors of ethical wills reflect on their past, take stock of who they are in the present and project into the future with their hopes, wishes and requests.

If you choose to create a journal, know that this involves writing things down regularly over a period of weeks, months, or even years. This method is an unstructured and spontaneous way to write about events, thoughts and feelings that strike you as important, and possibly to discover what you really think or feel about a given situation, relationship, or experience.

Linking the Past, Present and Future

From the past:

- Meaningful personal or family stories, passed down from previous generations.

- Family history — for multinational families, where did the family members originate?

- Lessons learned from personal or familial experience.

- Regrets.

From the present:

- Personal values and beliefs.

- Expressions of love and gratitude.

- Apologies.

For the future:

- Blessings, dreams, and hopes for the world, for future generations.

- Advice and guidance.

- Requests.

Things to Remember

Be yourself. You're not trying to win awards here. This is your chance to share with your current and future, extended family the person you are and how you hope to be remembered.

Keep in mind that your words are powerful. Certainly you want to be honest about your life experiences — both successes and failures — but negativity can be counterproductive and hurtful. Consider wisely what you commit to paper.

Composing your ethical will, although it may be difficult at first, it needn't be cumbersome or depressing. Think of it as another valuable gift you leave to your family. If it's hard for you to write, consider using a tape recorder or video camera, documenting your thoughts as they occur to you. When you've captured everything, you can replay it and type or write it down. You may even choose to have the final version on tape, DVD or video.

Take your time. Your personal legacy statement doesn't have to be written all at once. Feel free to revisit and redraft your ethical will as time passes and you learn and experience new things.

Consider sharing your personal legacy statement or ethical will with family members while you are able. You may find that you're glad you did, and you may even learn something about yourself, your life, and your legacy.

Cross-Border Philanthropy

Philanthropy, or in the original Greek, *philos anthropos*, means love of my fellow man. The practice of philanthropy by a family offers its members the opportunity to give to the outside world a portion of their time, talent, and wealth. Achieving your international philanthropic goals; however, can be a significant challenge. You may wish to give to a cause or charity in a country where you trace your family's ancestral roots or you may wish to benefit a global cause or a cause in a given country and aren't sure of the best conduit.

Whatever the situation, donors wanting to maximize the benefits of their giving typically have to cope with a lack of tax harmonization between countries. While a bequest to a charity located in your home country may not attract transfer tax, may provide a deduction against income tax or have estate-planning advantages, the same bequest to a charity, organization, or cause in another country may not. The issues of citizenship and residency apply in cross-border giving as it does in all other financial planning matters.

Some of the different taxes that might arise in a cross-border philanthropic operation are:

1. *Capital gains tax.* In some countries, the value of the assets transferred might be subject to a capital gains tax to be paid by the donor. If this is the case, the donor should determine if there are possibilities for exemption for charitable giving.

2. *Income tax.* Deduction of the gift. It should also be determined whether or not the value of the gift or donation can be deducted for income tax purposes. This deduction might depend on the domicile of the recipient versus the donor. In many cases, a deduction will not be available for cross-border operations.

3. *Corporate income tax.* In some countries, donations or gifts to legal entities are not subject to inheritance tax or gift taxes, but the recipient (charity or foundation) might be subject to some kind of corporate tax on the value of the asset received.

4. *Gift tax.* Lifetime gifts (e.g., donations and informal gifts) may be subject to gift tax, either payable by the donor or beneficiary, depending on the countries involved. In some countries, informal gifts may not be subject to tax provided that certain conditions are met.

5. *Inheritance taxes.* Upon receipt of a bequest, the beneficiary may have to pay tax on the value of the assets received Many countries grant exemption or reduced rates to public or charitable institutions.

6. *Estate taxes.* In some countries, the value of the decedent's estate might be subject to tax, reducing the proceeds available for beneficiaries.

7. *Transfer taxes.* Depending on the type of property being transferred, the donor or the beneficiary might be assessed transfer taxes on the property, perhaps on a local or national level.

For gift and inheritance taxes, relief is generally provided for donations or legacies to charities located in the same country as the donor, but might not be available for cross-border operations. For example, nonresident, non-U.S. citizens are allowed a charitable deduction on a U.S. Federal Estate Tax return, from the U.S. taxable assets, if the charity is either a U.S. charity or if the property is to be used only within the United States.

Additionally, nonresident, non-U.S. citizens can gift certain intangible assets, such as the securities of U.S. corporations, to others during their lifetime free of the U.S. gift tax. However, if this same person dies holding these assets, their estate is fully subject to tax. Of course, in cross-border planning any transfer taxes imposed by the home country of the person making the gift and the beneficiary of the gift, must also be considered before any gift is made.

In all cases, the donor and to the extent possible, the beneficiary, should ensure that the donation or gift or the donor's will, if the bequest takes place after the death of the donor, is valid and effective based on the legislation of the countries involved. In the true spirit of strategic planning, if you're the donor, you'll want to be sure that your advisors determine the likelihood that a gift or donation made today can or will be challenged.

There are many ways to give.

Donors can give directly to charity during their lifetime. Some countries provide tax relief for gifts to specific types of charities or under the condition of reciprocity. In certain cases, the impact of double taxation can be reduced or eliminated through deductions, exclusions, and tax credits. In addition, when inheritance tax or gift tax is the issue, donors and their advisors will also want determine if relief can be provided by an estate/inheritance, or gift tax treaty.

National private solutions or supporting organizations may also exist. Often these solutions have the characteristics of a public charity and a private foundation and are located in the donor's country of residence. This entity is able to collaborate with the intended foreign beneficiary and to receive, in a tax-effective way, the gift. For example, many charitable organizations interested in raising funds from American citizens have created an entity known as "The American Friends of…." This entity meets the guidelines for a U.S. charity and therefore allows a U.S. citizen to make a tax-deductible gift to their chosen cause.

Another private solution includes the donor advised fund. A donor advised fund is treated as a public charity and allows the donor to advise on how he or she would like grants to be made using the money he or she has gifted to the fund.

Multilateral private solutions may also exist in your region.

Families with sufficient financial assets to support their lifestyle and wealth transfer goals and who have a strong interest in promoting their social capital goals may wish to create a formal organization to support their philanthropic endeavors. The benefits of these structures (versus a direct gift) may include a tax-advantaged environment in which to grow the gifted assets, an efficient vehicle for portfolio diversification, and a mechanism for leveraging multi-generational giving and the notion of legacy.

The form of organization should be determined in consultation with your team of cross-border advisors, but at a minimum, the following broad options may be considered: (1) a fixed dollar amount to heirs, with the remainder to charity, (2) a specific dollar amount to charity, with the remainder to heirs, (3) a fixed percentage of wealth to heirs, with the remainder to heirs and (4) a fixed percentage of wealth to charity, with the remainder to heirs.

Before I move into the benefits of a private foundation, it's important to note that the theme of different laws continues. As noted above, a foundation may be created via incorporation of a company or via settlement of a trust. I have already introduced the challenges that trusts face internationally which has an impact on the structure used to carry out your philanthropic wishes. For example, the concept of the foundation is recognized by French law (*fondation*); however, it is limited in the work it can carry out. In Sweden a foundation (*stifstelse*) may be created for charitable purposes, but it meets with a more aggressive tax environment if it's established for family purposes. Indian law does not know the concept of a foundation. As with all cross-border planning, the majority of work must center on setting clear goals and objectives, so that the opportunities and challenges presented in each jurisdiction involved in the planning sphere may be analyzed to clear the path for the development of an appropriate strategy.

The Private Foundation

A private foundation is a charity that is founded and controlled by an individual or a family. A private foundation may be set up as a not-for-profit corporation or as a trust, and offers its founder the ability to make a difference in the world, build a permanent legacy, gain personal satisfaction and recognition and keep control in the family.

Making a Difference

Whether you or your family decides to volunteer your time, give directly to various causes or create any number of private structures, your social capital is much more than a sum of money set aside for philanthropic use. It's the carefully cultivated, ever-evolving product of you and your family's vision and interest. The strategies used to make a difference are as varied and interesting as the internationally mobile people and their families, who inspired them.

Transmitting Values

Not only can parents or grandparents leave money to heirs, they can leave something that can't be taxed, dissipated, or lost to bad investments: values. As Lynn Astinof wrote in the *Wall Street Journal*: "If your real goal is to transmit your values as well as your wealth, you can't wait until you're dead." Similarly, the values transmitted to your children will prepare them to live their own lives, carry out their visions of success and carry on the family's philanthropic vision after you are gone.

15

CROSS-BORDER DIVORCE

When the Marriage Turns Sour

Although it can be argued that you don't plan in advance to divorce your spouse, it's critical that internationally mobile people consider the various laws that may affect them. There is no global consensus on how best to divide the assets of divorcing couples and there are sharp differences between the divorce laws and practices of different countries. Yet very few people do their homework on these critical issues at a time when it could really make a big difference, assuming that wherever they live is necessarily the jurisdiction in which they must bring a divorce.

Despite the increased sophistication of international finance, family laws around the world are interwoven with local culture, religion, and history and change at a much slower pace than society in general. While the model of a family unit with a single local permanent residency is becoming outmoded, divorce laws generally remain tied to the idea that married couples belong to one certain place that will resolve the legal aspects of their relationship.

Procedural Differences and Choice of Law Rules

Not only do different countries' laws differ as they appear on the statute books, but the practices and procedures can differ in ways that *dramatically* affect the result. It's important to understand how this may affect your financial and life plan, and also be sure that you find appropriate counsel.

It will be important to note when financial matters are handled. For example, is a divorce decree issued prior to or after resolution surrounding financial matters? This will differ across jurisdictions.

It's also important to note that many countries have specific code or statutory provisions concerning the choice of law.

For guidance purposes, examples of differences of jurisdictional issues are provided below. As noted throughout the book, specific guidance from qualified professionals will be required.

CANADA: A Canadian court is a specific Canadian province has jurisdiction in a divorce proceeding if one spouse has been ordinarily resident in the province for one year before filing.

BERMUDA: Bermuda courts have jurisdiction if either party (1) is domiciled in Bermuda or (2) was ordinarily resident in Bermuda for one year before filing.

ENGLAND: Courts in England and Wales have jurisdiction if either spouse (1) is domiciled in England or Wales or (2) has been habitually resident in England and Wales for one year prior to filing.

MEXICO: Competent court is the court of matrimonial domicile or, in case of abandonment, the domicile of the abandoned party. Domicile implies permanent rather than temporary residence.

GERMANY: German courts have personal jurisdiction if, (1) one spouse is German or (2) the wife at the time of marriage was German or (3) if both spouses are aliens, at least one of them resides in Germany, provided that a divorce decree will be recognized by laws governing the husband.

KOREA: In Korea, in the case of adultery, which is a serious crime there, the law is enforced both in civil and criminal courts. In divorce cases the "innocent" spouse may receive substantial monetary compensation from the spouse who is found guilty of adultery. In addition, the criminal court may impose serious penalties, including imprisonment, for adultery.

THE PHILIPPINES: Divorce is prohibited in the Philippines. However, a section of the Family Code provides that a marriage can be voided if one of the contracting parties is psychologically incapacitated to perform the essential marital obligations, even if this incapacity surfaces only after the marriage is contracted. A divorce decree obtained in another country, on the initiative of a Philippine citizen, is not recognized or considered valid in the Philippines. An alien spouse; however, may obtain a divorce outside of the Philippines, which will be recognized in the Philippines.

International divorce raises the issue of where the divorce should be pursued. Although in many cases there may not be any choice about the jurisdiction in which the divorce is carried out, in certain cases a choice is available. Either way, it may be worth determining in advance the various possibilities.

Movement of Children Across Borders

Serious problems can arise when parental abduction results in moving a child, with a parent, across an international border. The laws of the states are different, and a foreign child custody order may not be recognized.

The Hague Convention on the Civil Aspects of International Child Abduction is an international treaty and legal mechanism to recover children abducted to another country by one parent or family member. The United States signed this into law in 1988. Japan is the only G7 nation that has not signed this treaty into law.

The Hague Convention on the Civil Aspects of International Child Abduction is a multilateral treaty developed by the Hague Conference on Private International Law that provides an expeditious method to return a child taken from one member nation to another. Proceedings on the Convention concluded on 25 October, 1980 and the Convention entered into force between the signatory nations on 1 December 1983. The Convention was drafted to "insure the prompt return of children who have been abducted from their country of habitual residence or wrongfully retained in a contracting state not their country of habitual residence." [22] The Hague Convention seeks "to protect children internationally from the harmful effects of their wrongful removal or retention and to establish procedures to ensure their prompt return to the state of their habitual residence, as well as to secure protection for the rights of access." [23] The primary intention of the Convention is to preserve whatever status quo child custody arrangement existed immediately before an alleged wrongful removal or retention thereby deterring a parent from crossing international boundaries in search of a more sympathetic court. The Convention applies only to children under the age of sixteen.

Pre-Divorce Planning Checklist

If you are contemplating divorce and believe that given your circumstances, the divorce may be carried out in more than one jurisdiction, consider the following questions:

1. Which courts have jurisdiction and what law will they apply? While you may be a citizen of a given country, doesn't necessarily mean that you will be able to take your divorce case there. Some countries require residency.

2. In other countries, such as Japan, divorce law is based, in significant part, on nationality. A Japanese court will apply Japanese law if the parties are Japanese. But what if they are citizens of different countries? According to Jeremy Morley, in

---

this situation, "the Japanese court will apply the law of the place of their residence if they habitually reside in the same place; otherwise it will use the law of the place that is most closely associated with the parties. In the case of a Japanese citizen married to a non-Japanese citizen, the Japanese court will use Japanese law if the Japanese citizen habitually resides in Japan."

3. Is there anything that you can do that will give a court jurisdiction, such as by moving back to your home country permanently or at least for a while? How can you do this effectively? What are the risks?

4. How do the different courts define the term "assets"? Which are subject to being divided? You will need to identify the assets that you and your spouse now own and group them into categories including: (1) items owned prior to your marriage, (2) items acquired during the marriage, (3) items received as an inheritance and other variables that you can think of. In addition, note where these assets are physically held or located and the existence of any trusts.

5. What are the criteria that the respective courts use to divide the assets? For example, do the courts look at what is equitable? Or do the courts look at the needs of the parties? What is the likely impact of the approach that is expected to be enforced?

6. What are the rules for maintenance or alimony? How are they applied?

7. What are the grounds for divorce? How does the jurisdiction handle this?

8. If you have children, what are the rules concerning custody and support of children? Jurisdictions around the world vary enormously in their treatment of children upon a divorce. Issues include:

- Sole custody versus joint custody

- Male-dominated approaches versus female-dominated approaches

- Visitation rights to non-custodial parent

- Religious biases versus impartiality

- National biases versus impartiality

- Freedom to relocate

- Freedom to take children overseas

Pre- and Post-Nuptial Agreements

Pre- and post-nuptial agreements can be an important planning tool for people of different nationalities who plan to wed and in situations where a married couple will reside overseas or for people who maintain property in various jurisdictions. One must consider the impact of different jurisdictions in the event of a divorce and therefore one term of international pre- and post-nuptial agreements that is often of critical significance is the choice of law clause.

It must be recognized that not all jurisdictions will allow these agreements to be enforced and that the requirements for pre- and post-nuptial agreements to be valid vary also among international jurisdictions and to some extent, within jurisdictions of countries.

Prenuptial agreements may also be used as estate planning devices.

Trust Assets

Jurisdictions vary considerably in their treatment of assets placed in trust. Some jurisdictions will "look through" or "pierce" the trust. Others will not.

Inherited Assets

Many jurisdictions do not divide assets that a spouse has received as an inheritance. Others, (the Netherlands, for example), do.

Top Ten Tips from an International Family Lawyer[24]

1. Before you move overseas, realize that if you have children in a new country you may find yourself trapped there. For example, Angie the American and Gus the Greek (from Cyprus) moved to Cyprus with their baby. Life in Cyprus didn't work out for Angie. In fact, she hates it there. But Gus refuses to leave and he refuses to allow Angie to take the baby back to the U.S. to live. Since both Cyprus and the U.S. are parties to The Hague Convention on the Civil Aspects of International Child Abduction, Angie will be in big trouble if she takes the child back to the U.S. without Gus' permission.

2. If you make a deal with your husband or wife that you're going overseas just for a trial and that you'll return if it doesn't work out — get it in writing. Verbal agreements always seem to be forgotten when things blow up. But also know that even a written agreement may not work. A foreign court handling your child custody case may well decide that it doesn't care what your deal was with the other parent; it must only consider what is best for the kids.

---

[24] This section is a re-print with permission of an article written by Jeremy D. Morley. Mr. Morley may be reached at 212-372-3425 and through his website, www.international-divorce.com. He handles international divorce, international child abduction and other international family law matters in New York and, with local counsel, around the world. He has taught in law schools in England, Illinois and Canada, has lived in Japan, and has done business in more than 20 countries in Europe, Asia and South America.

3. Before you switch residences, consider how it might impact a possible divorce. For example, Arnie and Alice in America signed a prenuptial agreement before they married. Not only that, but Arnie made pretty sure that it was watertight not only by having it drafted by his own lawyer, but also by insisting that Alice have her own independent lawyer, and by putting terms in the agreement that are pretty fair to Alice. Arnie feels secure. Then they move to London, England, oblivious of the fact that their prenuptial agreement may well be unenforceable in a divorce court in England. English courts still hold that prenuptial agreements are against public policy and, while this policy is supposed to be changing, it most certainly hasn't changed yet. To make matters much worse for Arnie (who had bags of money before the marriage and thought he was fully protected by the prenuptial agreement), there is no distinction in England between marital property and separate property acquired before the marriage. He could be blowing half of his pre-marriage assets just by moving the family to England.

4. Before leaving home, you should hope and plan for the very best. But you should also be prepared for the very worst. So, if you are a "trailing spouse" be sure to consider the following:

   • Don't sell the house. If you maintain an address in your home country it may be easier to claim that you maintained your home as your permanent residence. Certainly it will indicate that it continues to be your "domicile" (the place you live in indefinitely which remains as your domicile even if you move temporarily to another place remains your home). Having a place to return to will also make your case a lot stronger if you need to prove that your kids should be allowed to move "back home."

- Keep your contacts with your job. Prepare for the day when you may want to re-enter the job market back home. Perhaps you can continue to do some work even while overseas.

- Keep your network of friends and family at home.

5. If you're overseas and are "planning" to get divorced, be as strategic as possible. Plan your moves. Consult someone who really understands the big picture. Figure out where it's best for you to be at the time you tell your soon-to-be-ex that it's all over. You may need to move yourself, the kids, the soon-to-be-ex and the marital assets to another place before you break the news that you want out of the marriage. And don't leave without the evidence. Intelligent planning, with strategic professional advice, is the key.

6. If you're feeling stuck overseas and have children with you, don't just bolt for the (airplane) door with the kids and run "back home" to (the States). Plan things out first. If you take the kids you may be guilty of international child kidnapping. You could even be arrested at the airport before you leave. If you make it to (the States), you'll probably be forced to return by an American court — and then, to completely add insult to injury, you'll probably have to pay your spouse's legal fees and travel expenses as well as your own. When you return your case will be heard in the foreign court, where you will be branded as an international child abductor. Consult knowledgeable international family law counsel sooner, rather than later.

7. On the other hand, if it's your spouse who's feeling unhappy and upset and who may "do a runner" back home, there are lots of things that *you* should be doing. Some are pretty obvious: be kind; be understanding and don't stay out all night with the guys or gals from the office. Other tips are not so clear, and whether you implement them depends very much on the circumstances.

Hide the passports. Befriend his or her travel agent, who may tell you if he or she is making an airline reservation. Consult his or her friends. Suggest counseling. Have a plan to call the police and alert the border guards if you discover that he or she has taken the kids.

8. If you're overseas and pregnant, and not 1000% percent confident that you'll always want to live in the overseas country, consider very seriously getting out of there now. If your baby is born overseas, whether in Sweden or Saudi Arabia, the child's "habitual residence" for purposes of The Hague Convention will be Sweden or Saudi Arabia — and that can create terrible problems for you if you want to take your baby "back home."

9. Don't assume that the local authorities won't help. So many times, expats feel that the local social welfare agencies won't understand and will automatically side with the other spouse who is a citizen (of that country). In fact, in many countries the support services are excellent and you should try them. Plus, an American court in a Hague Convention case won't accept your defense that returning a child to the foreign country will put the child in grave risk of harm unless you can show that the foreign support services are unable to provide the needed protection.

10. Local divorce lawyers may not be your best bet. They want your business. They have an incentive to encourage you to bring your lawsuit in the place where they practice and they usually don't know anything about the laws in other places. An international divorce lawyer, who consults with local lawyers as appropriate, can give you much more objective "big-picture" advice.

A Final Word on Cross-Border Divorce

A divorce can be emotionally and financially devastating. At the first sign of real trouble, be sure to seek advice from someone who can help you navigate all of the varied issues and put you in touch with appropriate resources. Over the years that I've been in practice, I've helped steer families to counseling programs, through mediation and served as an independent, third party to prepare the financial impact to proposed settlements. One thing I've learned from these experiences is that anger gets you nowhere. The more a spouse seeks personal revenge through the divorce settlement process, the more likely the process is to be more expensive and destructive. The financial and emotional healing process is also likely to be longer.

16
CROSS-BORDER ENTREPRENEURS

As I noted back in Chapter 1, today it is easier to work on your own terms from just about anywhere in the world. Technological and digital advances have given us a global reach and more time, more freedom, and more options for a globally mobile lifestyle.

Whether a solo run professional services firm, a start-up or the family owned and operated business that has expanded exponentially over several generations, you may operate in more than one country and thus touch at least two tax systems.

Many of the jurisdictional issues presented in this book also pertain to businesses. The type of structure to use in a given jurisdiction, ownership restrictions, depending on nationality and the intersection of local law, the use of subsidiary companies and or agents in another country, the possibility for withholding on income earned in various jurisdictions, all add another layer of complexity that must be explored with specialist corporate advisors.

In this chapter we'll look quickly at some of the tactical tax and reporting issues for those with connections to the United States. It bears repeating here that H.R. 1, originally known as the "Tax Cuts and Jobs Act" signed into law in late 2017, includes substantial changes to the taxation of individuals and businesses. Certain of the tax law provisions are mentioned below; however, much of this is still subject to further interpretation once guidance is issued by Treasury, regulations or future technical corrections. Thus, as with all reference to this Act, the guidance listed here is strictly preliminary.

After we cover some of these tax and reporting issues and how some of them are changing, we'll circle back to strategic level planning issues for business owners, because the chances are high that the definitional lines that separate you and/or your family from the business are blurred or overlap. Let's dive in to those technical issues now.

Business owners with connections to the United States may have several additional filing requirements depending on the type of company that you establish, and where it is established, among other things. Let's take a closer look.

Special Foreign Earned Income Exclusion Rules Apply to Self-Employed Individuals

If you are self-employed and living abroad, you may find that the foreign earned income and foreign housing cost exclusions are less advantageous and more complex for you than they are for employees.

While the principles of qualifying for the foreign earned income exclusion are the same, whether you are self-employed or an employee, there may be some limitation on the amount that you can claim as foreign earned income.

The foreign earned income exclusion (FEIE) is applied to your income before expenses (e.g. your gross receipts). If your business provides personal services, such as legal services, and you are self-employed, all of your income is characterized as "earned." If this is not the case, the amount of your gross receipts that can be characterized as earned cannot exceed 30% of the net profits of your business. Therefore, in many cases, this may mean that the maximum allowable FEIE is less than the annual maximum (USD 102,100 for 2017 and USD 104,100 for 2018).

Disallowance of Business Expenses

The so-called "denial of double benefits rule" prevents you from claiming a deduction for expenses that are related to excluded income; therefore, if you are self-employed and claim the foreign earned income exclusion against some of your gross receipts, a portion of your business expenses will not be allowed. Because the foreign earned income exclusion is applied to gross receipts rather than net income, it may be less beneficial to you than it would be to an employee.

For example, Tom, Susan, and Phil are U.S. citizens who live abroad and qualify for the foreign earned income exclusion for all of 2017. Tom is a salaried employee, Susan is a self-employed accountant, and Phil is a self-employed manufacturer and distributor of bracelets. Each of them has USD 110,300 of net employment income after expenses.

All Figures USD	Tom: Salaried employee	Susan: Self-employed accountant	Phil: Self-employed manufacturer
Gross Income	110,300	170,300	260,300
Business Expenses	0	(60,000)	(150,000)
Net Income	110,300	110,300	110,300
FEIE	102,100	102,100	33,090*
Disallowed Expenses:	0	(102,100/170,300 x 60,000) = 35,972	(33,090/260,300 x 150,000) = 19,068

Calculation of Taxable Earnings:			
Gross Income	110,300	170,300	260,300
FEIE	(102,100)	(102,100)	(33,090)
Taxable Gross Income	8,200	68,200	227,210
Business Expenses	n/a	60,000	150,000
Disallowed Expenses	n/a	(35,972)	19,068
Allowable Expenses	n/a	24,028	130,932
Net Taxable Earnings	8,200	44,172	96,278

* Limited to "reasonable earned income," up to a maximum of 30% of net income. In the example this is calculated as follows: (110,300 x 30% = 33,090).

Business expenses when thought through in the context of your *Cross Border Life + Wealth Achievement Plan* can have a significant positive impact even if a portion of them are disallowed. It pays to keep excellent records and know the rules that affect business expenses.

Tax Deductible Business Expenses

Space does not permit me to go into detail here; however, some specific areas you will want to understand include: travel, meals, house expenses, and education expenses.

Overall, this is an area where your business plan and your *Cross-Border Life + Wealth Achievement Plan* will want to align, because in order to have a business deduction, we need to meet three tests: 1) it has to have a business purpose, 2) it is typical for your type of business and 3) it is necessary. That means does it help create a profit, help you increase market share, increase sales? Keep these in mind as you consider strategy within the business to achieve the business goals (which, in turn, assist in the achievement of your *Cross-Border Life + Wealth Achievement Plan.*

Another common area of confusion is how self-employed individuals use foreign housing costs. We'll look at that now, followed by issues associated with U.S. self-employment tax.

Foreign Housing Cost Deduction

If you are self-employed, you're not allowed to claim the foreign housing cost exclusion. Instead, you can claim a deduction (known as the "foreign housing cost deduction") that is calculated the same way as the foreign housing cost exclusion. This foreign housing cost deduction is limited to the amount of foreign earned income that you have in excess of the foreign earned income exclusion. Because of the way that the stacking rule and the denial of double benefits rule, (which I have not covered in detail), work, in some cases, the foreign housing cost deduction may be more advantageous than the foreign housing cost exclusion that you would be entitled to if you were an employee.

Self-Employment Tax

As a U.S. self-employed person, you must continue to pay self-employment tax (FICA[25]) even when you are living abroad, and even if you are paying social security tax in your country of residence. Net earnings subject to self-employment tax are figured without taking the FEIE into consideration.

---

[25] FICA, or Federal Insurance Contributions Act, refers to U.S. Social Security and Medicare taxation.

If you are self-employed and working in a country that has a social security totalization agreement with the United States, you may be exempt from self-employment tax. For more information regarding how to determine if one of these agreements applies to you, refer to the United States Social Security Administration Web site (www.ssa.gov/international).

Otherwise, the self-employment tax rate is 15.3 percent of net earnings up to a base amount (USD 127,200 in 2017 and USD 128,400 in 2018). In addition, earnings above the base amount are taxed at 2.9 percent, and earnings in excess of USD 200,000 (USD 250,000 for joint earnings of a married couple filing jointly) are subject to an additional 0.9 percent tax, to total 3.8 percent.

Partnerships

If you are a service provider in a service partnership, you are considered to be self-employed for U.S. tax purposes. This means that you are subject to self-employment tax and your foreign earned income exclusion is calculated as mentioned earlier. Generally, you must look to the proportion of the partnership income as a whole that was earned outside the United States, rather than what proportion of your services were provided outside the United States, when determining the portion of your partnership income that can be considered foreign earned income. This means that even if you are a partner who works exclusively outside the United States, but your partnership earns income in the United States, a portion of your partnership income will not be eligible for the foreign earned income exclusion. The rules may be different; however, if you receive a "guaranteed payment," or if you receive a special allocation of overseas profits from the partnership.

If you are a partner in a foreign partnership, the rules regarding taxation of your partnership income are the same as mentioned above; however, there are special reporting requirements for U.S. partners of foreign partnerships on Form 8865, *Return of U.S. Persons with Respect to Certain Foreign Partnerships*.

You may decide that you want to incorporate a non-U.S. company for any number of legal or business reasons, but you want it treated for U.S. tax purposes as a sole proprietorship. In this case you will need to file Form 8832, *Entity Classification Election* to elect tax treatment as an "entity disregarded as separate from its owner."

If you make this election, then you will also have to file Form 8858, *Information Return of U.S. Persons with Respect to Foreign Disregarded Entities*. This form will be filed together with your individual income tax return.

The 2017 Tax Act (H.R. 1) and Reduced Tax Rate on Income from "Pass-Through" Entities

In this section we have been focused on businesses that are referred to as "pass-through" entities such as sole proprietorship, S corporation or partnership. If you're running your business via one of these structures and you're a U.S. citizen or resident, or you are a non-U.S. person that conducts business in the United States (e.g. you have so-called "effectively connected income"), then you are probably aware of the new 20% deduction on qualified business income that came into being. A detailed explanation of this new legislation is beyond the scope of this book as is the answer to how best to structure your business across borders. However, I will address a couple of key basic issues to reduce some early areas of confusion:

- First, note that "qualified business income" is from conduct of trades and businesses within the United States only.[26]

- Generally, the term "qualified business income" means the net of qualified items of income, gain, deduction, and loss with respect to any of your qualified trades or businesses.[27] Note this includes rental income and also note that there are exclusions to this definition including but not limited to various types of investment income as well as compensation income.

- Under the new Section 199A of the tax code, the favorable 20 percent of qualified business income deduction can be phased in or phased out depending on your taxable income, beginning with tax years after December 31, 2017.

- Some rules apply to what Section 199A calls a "specified service trade or business", such as operating as a law or accounting firm. But if the person operating this type of business has defined taxable income less than certain thresholds, he or she can still qualify for the full 20 percent deduction on his or her qualified business income.

Non-US Corporations

When you become an owner, officer or director of a company incorporated outside the United States ("foreign corporation"), it is important to be aware that you may need to include a special information report with your annual tax return, Form 5471, *Information Return of U.S. Persons with Respect to Certain Foreign Corporations*. The form applies to several categories of individuals, and the information that must be reported varies depending on which category you are in.

---

[26] IRC Section 199A(c)(3)(A).
[27] IRC Section 199A(c)(1).

The Tax Act of 2017 (H.R. 1) made changes that impact tax years of foreign corporations that begin after December 31, 2017 and tax years of U.S. shareholders in which or with which such tax years of foreign corporations end.

Generally, under pre-Act rules, a foreign corporation itself, if it's not doing business in the United States and if it does not have a U.S. source income, is not taxable in the United States. Shareholders are taxable on compensation and dividend distributions.

Distributions from these foreign corporations can be ordinary dividends, qualified dividends or something called "deemed distributions of Subpart F income."

Subpart F refers to a section of the Internal Revenue Code that was designed to prevent deferral of passive income inside a foreign corporation that can be classified as closely held by U.S. persons. Closely held for these purposes is defined as a corporation where more than 50% of the value or voting power is owned by U.S. shareholders. In this situation, tax is assessed against the "U.S. shareholder" of the foreign corporation, not the corporation itself and not all U.S. persons who own shares in the closely held foreign corporation are subject to tax on the corporation's income. Only those shareholders who own, directly or indirectly, 10% or more of the corporation's voting power are considered U.S. shareholders and are therefore subject to tax on certain kinds of the foreign corporation's income, whether or not the corporation makes a distribution to the U.S. shareholder.

Two of the categories of income classified as Subpart F income include passive items of income ("Foreign Personal Holding Company Income (FPHC))," and income derived from services by the company for, or on behalf of, a related party that are performed outside of the country in which the corporation is incorporated ("Foreign Base Company Income (FBCI)." FPHC income generally consists of dividends, interest, royalties, rent, annuities, gains on dispositions of property generating other types of foreign income, net gains from certain commodities transactions, net foreign currency gains, income equivalent to interest, income from notional contracts, payments in lieu of dividends, and income from certain personal service contracts, unless there is an exception.

New Territorial Taxation of Corporations Provisions

Under the new rules, "U.S. shareholder" means a United States person who owns 10 percent or more of the total combined voting power of all classes of stock entitled to vote of such foreign corporation, or 10 percent or more of the total value of shares of all classes of stock of such foreign corporation.[28] So beginning with 2018, you are a United States shareholder if you hold 10% or more of either the voting power or the value of the corporation.

In addition, any accumulated foreign earnings of "Controlled Foreign Corporations" will now be deemed as having been repatriated to the United States and therefore will be taxed as a U.S. federal rate of 15.5% for cash and cash equivalents, or at 8% for illiquid assets.

While taxpayers can elect to pay this tax over an eight-year period it is still a new tax challenge for owners of small foreign companies.

Additional changes include imposing a current tax, similar to subpart F, on a U.S. shareholder's "global intangible low-taxed income" of a controlled foreign corporation, and modification of certain aspects of the "subpart F" anti-deferral rules.

***

---

[28] IRC Section 951(b) (2018).

While tax law, business law, cultures, and business practices differ across the globe, the human elements and challenges faced by businesses with cross-border elements are often similar. Now that we've covered quite a bit of the tactical issues that your Cross-Border Life + Wealth Achievement Plan may consider, let's close out this chapter and this section of the book to consider some special additional planning levels that come with entrepreneurship.

We'll start by looking at an important question:

How Does Your Business Fit With Your Personal And Family Vision, Purpose, and Mission?

Your business may be the most important vehicle through which you can achieve your vision, purpose, and mission, if it's to contribute to achieving the life and lifestyle you are designing. It therefore requires a strategy to help you direct the business in such a way that it supports your personal, social and financial dimensions of wealth.

It can happen in either of two ways: You could choose to develop your business in such a way that it frees you to pursue other interests, or the business could itself be a reflection of the very essence of what's most important to you.

When we are planning at this level there are three systems that we need to keep in mind. Once we understand these systems, we can use them as context as we create the various strategic plans we need to achieve our vision, purpose and/or mission.

The 3 Systems

Generally we must recognize that there are three systems (the family system, the ownership system, and the business system), through which business goals and outcomes can be expressed to support your goals within the social, financial, and personal dimensions of wealth.

Family System. The family system is made up of your family members. Most goals are inward looking and are based on emotion.

Ownership System. This system is made up of all shareholders of the company, whether family or not. The goals are typically forward looking and profit driven.

Business System. The business system is made up of the management, employees, and customers/clients of the business. Its focus is typically on meeting the needs of its customers/clients and therefore is task-oriented.

THE 3 SYSTEMS

You may hold membership in one or all of these systems, each with its own unique perspective. The areas of overlap between systems help to illustrate where potential issues of confusion, conflict, and differing perspectives arise.

Referring to the illustration above, these areas of overlap are labeled according to the first letter of the related systems. At the center of the diagram, labeled FOB, are people who are family members, owners and who are involved at some level in the business. This may include one or more founders of the business as well as family members who have inherited or been given shares. Each member of this group is more susceptible to feelings of confusion or conflict between and across the three unique perspectives that they possess in this position. It's also possible that the boundaries between family, ownership, and business become blurred.

The area labeled FB is made up of family members who do not own shares in the business, but who work in the business. The area where the ownership system and the family system, labeled FO, represents family members who are an owner in the business, but who do not work in the business. This may include passive shareholders like children or spouses who inherit ownership in the business, but who do not actively participate in its daily operations. Last, employees who are not members of the family may also be owners. This area of perspective and overlap is labeled OB.

Each of these systems has differing wants and needs. Vision may also be different among the groups. Understanding the dynamics at work in your situation begins with defining the membership of each of these systems, the current role that they play (or don't play), and any messages or cultural barriers that must be taken into consideration.

For example, I worked with a family whose in which the patriarch and founder of the business, had died, leaving his spouse ownership of the company. She had never been directly involved in the running of the business and had grown up believing that women did not "belong" in business. While she believed this pertained to her situation, she allowed her daughters to get involved. When I entered the picture, I found one of the son's in law (a member, along with his wife, of the FB group) running the company and feeling very frustrated by the fact that the owner would not transfer ownership to the daughters, or put money into the business. In fact, the wife and matriarch of this family (the sole member of the FOB group) would not address many of the issues facing her family. A further complication to this situation involved the cross-border nature of the family and the business. There were three nationalities involved, most of the family members were dual citizens and the family owned real property in more than one country. Their family lawyer had been trying for years to assist, but the various money messages running through the matriarch's mind caused her to put the brakes on any plan that upset the status quo.

Effective Planning Involves Each Stakeholder

When I consulted with the family in the situation highlighted above, my first task was to spend time with the matriarch to help her see her family in the context of the systems diagram. Once she understood the context from which the concerns being expressed by certain stakeholders originated, I was able to show her how we might design a plan that would align the needs and goals of each stakeholder — in this case the matriarch, the company, the matriarch's adult children and their families.

The Alignment Process

The planning components that must be aligned are the owner's plan, the family plan, the company plan and the succession plan. As already addressed in the first section of this book, for each plan there is a human/personal and financial element. In addition, the family, owner and company plan may include a social element. We discussed that the human/ personal element is concerned with balancing personal goals, relationships, community, living through values, communication, and other facets of daily living. It's also concerned with carrying out the family and/or personal mission statement, whether we formally express it or not.

Similarly, consideration of the various economic and other financial issues is given for each plan.

For first generation business owners, the planning components that require alignment are the owner's plan, the company plan and, assuming the goal is to see the company ownership extend beyond the founder or provide liquidity for the family, the succession plan. Once ownership extends to additional family members and non-family members or partners, the family plan is particularly useful.

The Owner's Plan. Most of the content of this book has already addressed most of the issues related to the owner's personal financial plan that should be addressed, as well as how the owner's plan relates to the goals and vision of the other family members and the family plan; therefore I will not repeat this information here. Other areas for consideration in the owner's plan; however, include the owner's role, now and in the future, and the role of the company or business as seen by the owner. By the time the owner has addressed his or her personal goals, roles for the future and the social and financial dimensions of their life and wealth, the exit or succession goal has also been established.

The Family Plan. The issues facing a family and the plans for responding to the various issues are constantly evolving. As a result, the reality of the family plan is that it's a continuing process of review and communication, carried out through regular meetings. Although the mission of the business, leadership and governance issues, and the rights and obligations of family members are some of the standard areas the family plan might address, operational issues are not the only issues that this planning process might tackle. As outlined in Chapter Three, a successful planning process is also about understanding the perspectives of individual family members, the development and implementation of shared family goals, and the development of individual family members. One important benefit of the family plan for business owners and families without businesses is that it allows individual family members to move forward in their own careers and lives as they see fit. The plan allows them to view the map and where they fit in. It provides them with the direction they can use to create a life and financial plan of their own.

The Company/Business Plan. The only difference between a company or business plan that is closely held and one that is not, is the fact that in the case of the closely held business, it is integral to the success of its owners and their families. As a result, the company plan and the metrics designed to measure the success of the company must be viewed in the context of the requirements set out by the owner and family plans. Specific questions to be addressed include:

- Does the business plan meet the needs of the personal financial plan?

- How do the personal and family goals translate into business goals?

- If the business cannot meet the needs, what needs to change?

- What are the milestones that indicate that the plan is on schedule or behind schedule?

The Succession Plan. The succession plan sets out the exit or succession goal and examines the impact of the plan on the owner(s), the family, and the business, with a view toward facilitating the effective and efficient transfer of ownership, leadership, and wealth. It illustrates the net effect, incorporating tax and other considerations into the model. By measuring the impact on the family goals, alternatives can be evaluated and goals refined as necessary. Once the preliminary plan is developed it must be communicated and modified as necessary, over time. One of the benefits of succession planning is that it brings families together, while *not* planning often drives them apart. Succession plans allow both the senior and next generation to proceed with their own lives, free of uncertainty. Whether the business is to be sold or is to stay in the family, a succession plan helps owners arrive at the best choice for everyone and helps family members plan their own lives.

Although each of these plans can be prepared independently of one another, the ideal process starts with the assumption of an existing business plan. If a company or business plan is not in place then it will be important to ensure that a formal business strategy is developed and articulated. This is important because the issues and assumptions articulated in the plan are used to define the priorities of the business. These priorities can be projected over time and analyzed to determine if they are mutually reinforcing or competing. With the business/company's strategy clearly defined, we can evaluate how well the business will support the owner plan and family goals now and over the projected time frame.

The process begins by addressing the owner's plan, followed by addressing the goals of the family members and other shareholders, to eventually develop a family plan. This event is closely followed, or even simultaneously, by the company or business plan, and succession plan.

It is often the case that the goals expressed by the individual/ owner, family and company plans to clash with one another. For example, there is often "conflict" between the need of the company for additional capital, while the owner seeks to achieve or maintain financial security, and family members seek to improve or maintain the lifestyle they are accustomed to. In most cases the financial resources are not available to achieve *all of these goals at the same time*. This reality supports the need for both *alignment of plans* and the need for families to take *an integrated approach* to their life and financial planning. Through discussion and tradeoffs a course of action can be mapped that addresses the goals and priorities of each stakeholder. In fact, the more comprehensive the approach and the sooner it is realized and put in place, the better.

There is a family, now in its third, fourth and fifth generations, with many individual members across the globe, which meets annually at a family meeting to reaffirm and readopt its family mission statement. Although the meeting agenda contains several items relating to cross-border financial matters, it's clear that the underlying primary purpose of the meeting is to remind family members who they are, where they come from, and the core values that drive the family.

This family demonstrates how a common set of values, goals, virtues, and understanding among its members leads to successful family wealth preservation over multiple generations and multiple jurisdictions.

CONCLUSION:
YOUR WORLD

We've come a long way. If I've successfully met my goals, then I hope you've learned enough to begin to overcome any overwhelm you may feel when it comes to tax and legal complexity. And I hope that you've felt inspired and empowered on how you can improve your life and your financial position across borders.

We've traveled far together, starting with an orientation for the journey itself. We discovered that the model of the Industrial Age couldn't work in the Information Age, so now we can be free of the deferred life plan based on a collection of socially reinforced illusions. This is empowering (and awesome) because today we live in a world in which globalization has moved from multi-national corporations to individuals. We no longer have to be limited to a single nation's economy. We can reduce our dependence on the existing market we are in, whether that's in our career, our life, or our business, because we *want* to. The global village we live in today allows us to consciously design a lifestyle that allows us to live, work, play, and make a difference *anywhere* in the world.

Our travels took us deep into understanding how we create wealth. We discovered the most powerful number we all possess — our human capital. We all have unique human capital in the form of skills, talents, knowledge, experience, and resources. We realized that what we have learned through our own journeys — our point of view — could be used to help people in the global village. By serving them, we can mine the best opportunities from all over the world and build for them and ourselves a true measure of time and financial freedom.

We've talked about what you should think about as you design a bigger, fuller vision for your life. We considered the question of, just how do we design a life that checks the boxes of your bucket list, stays true to your values and meets your future financial obligations and legacy?

We addressed the fact that while globalization takes place with ideas, the laws that govern immigration, taxation and succession are defined by national and municipal boundaries. Therefore, our financial planning *must* take the local customs and laws into consideration to make the most of the opportunities we seek to fulfill, without falling into any traps.

As I'm sure you know by now, this is not an easy journey. Like any journey into the unknown, it requires commitment and preparation. I don't know what circumstances allowed you to be reading these words at this moment, but I am honored that our paths have crossed and that I've been able to share what I've learned and figured out. I'm still learning and I'm still figuring it out. It's what we do as pioneers, as "expats", "lovepats", "triangles", "third country kids", "dual nationals" and all the other nouns that have been created over the years to help us understand this world, our places in it, and how we want to contribute to it.

Imagine a world where we could join innovation, capital, and thoughtful leadership to solve some of the world's biggest challenges. That is the global village. I believe in the global village and I believe that you have much to contribute to it, on *your* journey.

While the journey will challenge you, at least you now have a map, a methodology and some tools. I wish I had just some of this when I started my own journey into this world. What's left now is how do you use them, or obtain more specialized information from advisors or consultants to more fully implement them.

So what now?

If you haven't already done so, be sure to access the tools in our dedicated book resources vault and do the work. I also recommend that you build out your Life + Wealth Balance Sheet. That will require you to organize your financial information, which could take time. If you'd like to continue your learning or go deeper into this work, consider attending one of my events or joining one of my online learning programs. When you're ready just visit crossborderliving.com.

Over fifteen years ago, I saw through the complexity and uncertainty alongside the opportunities after my career and identity crisis. I learned that my questions were: Am I living where I want? Am I aligning my work with how I want to make a difference in the global village? Am I fulfilled personally? I didn't particularly like my answers to those questions, so I sought to change my life and to create a strategic plan to achieve it. It wasn't easy. I had to learn some new skills. But that striving ultimately led to the discovery of the model and methodology that we've talked so much about. This is about choice and intention. I hope that you can see that you have choices and that choices with some boundaries can contribute to a feeling of control, even when you can't see through the mist.

Thank you for allowing me the privilege of sharing my thoughts with you. As we say good-bye for now, I'd like to share one last piece that I hope you find inspiring. It's the *Cross-Border Couple Manifesto* and you'll find it in the End Note.

In the meantime, remember:

You're just one *Cross-Border Life + Wealth Achievement Plan* away...

END NOTE

The Cross-Border Couple Manifesto

It starts as an adventure. We're full of dreams. We feel in control. We know how we want our life to look. Our plan includes exploring the world while making our careers our priority. We are equal in so many ways. We're going to take on the world.

We start wanting a family. We go for it, and one of us takes a step...or two, backward in our career, telling ourselves that it will be temporary. We feel fortunate that our partner can take on the burden of being the main income earner for our family and our future. We trust our new plan. We are hopeful that nothing will go wrong.

We're busy with the children, the expectations, and trying to find time for one another in those early years. We think we're still on track with our plan to take on the world, although, in truth, we're not sure. We do know that we are still exploring the world with at least one career.

But each move leaves one of us further behind professionally, causing a re-evaluation and possibly a career reinvention. In every new location, local laws require navigation. Work permits must be obtained, legal documents reviewed, cash flow adjusted. Short-term moves limit the time for re-assessment. By the time we have adjusted to the new location, it becomes time to plan and execute the next move. Longer-term moves see us wrangling with the idea of buying real estate instead of renting, assuming that we are allowed to do so. Either way, we start losing touch with the adventure, and become more confused about the future – a future we know is coming, but we can't see through the mist of uncertainty.

We have a realization one day: A job does not define us, nor should it confine us. Being in a support role to the family does not mean that we can't have help. We realize we define ourselves, our relationship, and our future. Culture and family have a strong influence, but we are still at choice as to how we operate within, or from, that lens.

We consider the person we most want to be, or have to be, to get back to or stay on track with the plan we had when we started our journey. We inventory our skills, connections, passions, and interests and we discover that there are people worldwide who can learn from us, who can benefit from who or what we know. We begin to accept the identity of who we most want to be. It's both scary... and exhilarating. The energy spark conjures the memory of when we first decided to relocate overseas...to start our journey.

Some of us accept the calling of cross-border entrepreneurship, even if we decide as a couple that now is not the right time to set out. Some of us swap the role of family support for primary breadwinner with our partner, either as an entrepreneur or as a knowledge worker.

We stop limiting ourselves to the concept of "equal partners" favoring the concept of "equitable partners". We have access. The money that we and our partners earn – which we refer to as "our money" – buys us the location, financial and time freedom we both want. With equity, dependence is not in play. We have the signing authority we need and the credit we both need. We plan time together to design our next adventure or the next chapter of our lives together. We support one another in pursuing our individual goals, with our cultural and familial imprints around money, in the ebb and flow of our careers, with our roles, and as builders and stewards of our wealth.

The balance of power, perceived or real, is now transformed. The journey continues...

ABOUT THE AUTHOR

Jennifer A. Patterson believes that today, more than ever before, we can consciously design a lifestyle in which we live, work, play, and make a difference anywhere in the world, just because we *want* to. American by birth, Jennifer has personal experience with the life and technical financial planning opportunities and challenges faced by families with U.S. connections. She has lived overseas over half her life, thanks to her cross-cultural marriage, and is the proud mama of two tri-national kids: one applying to universities in various countries, while the other is a budding cross-border entrepreneur. An industry veteran, Jennifer is a CERTIFIED FINANCIAL PLANNER practitioner (CFP®), Certified Investment Management Analyst (CIMA™), and a Trust and Estate Practitioner (TEP). She has served in a volunteer leadership capacity for the U.S. based Financial Planning Association, as an international chapter founder for its predecessor organization, the International Association for Financial Planning and for a former associate member of the Financial Planning Standards Board.

After a career crisis in her early thirties brought on by her realization that all her industry related training in financial planning and investing—that the textbooks told her was all about helping people achieve their dreams—was in reality perpetuating the status quo of the Industrial Age sparked a life crisis, Jennifer faced what she calls the three core questions for life in the global village: Am I living where and how I want to? What's my contribution? And can I make a difference through my work or because of it? Her answers to those questions led to her previous book, *When Families Cross Borders: A Guide for Internationally Mobile People*, a groundbreaking work that was the first to address financial planning and wealth management for multinational families, dual citizens and the globally mobile.

It also led to the founding of Patterson Partners Ltd., an independent financial advisory firm specializing in cross-border tax and financial planning for families with U.S. connections, through which she has advised clients whose traditional balance sheet reflected net worth ranged from negative to tens of millions across multiple countries. Jennifer is now a recognized pioneer in cross-border wealth and life design. She founded the Global Institute for Life and Wealth to teach cross-border technical and practice related topics to practitioners and to run events and training for the globally mobile on how to create, grow, and manage financial assets in a way that most supports how we want to live our lives, globally. She is a frequent speaker and serves as the lead trainer for *Life + Wealth Weekend;* a weekend planning seminar for cross-border couples. Meet Jennifer at www.crossborderliving.com

ADDITIONAL TOOLS, RESOURCES AND INVITATIONS

The Expat Family File

http://www.theexpatlifeline.com/your-expat-family-file/

Done for you checklists and templates so you have the information you need, when you need it, wherever you are.

Life + Wealth Weekend for Cross-Border Couples

Two days in paradise where you'll create a plan that you both can agree on, while having fun. For more information visit www.crossborderliving.com.

Books

A. Martins and V. Hepworth, *Expat Women: Confessions – 50 Answers to Your Real-Life Questions about Living Abroad* (Expat Women Enterprises Pty Ltd ATF Expat Women Trust, 2011).

T. Carter and R. Yates, *Finding Home Abroad: A Guided Journal for Adapting to Life Overseas* (Summertime, 2014).

J. Heinzer, *Living Your Best Life Abroad: Resources, Tips and Tools for Women Accompanying Their Partners on an International Move* (Springtime Books, 2009).

L. Wiles and E. Simpson, *Thriving Abroad: The definitive guide to professional and personal relocation success* (Practical Inspiration Publishing, 2017).

L. Janssen, *The Emotionally Resilient Expat – Engage, Adapt and Thrive Across Cultures* (Summertime, 2013).

CPSIA information can be obtained
at www.ICGtesting.com
Printed in the USA
BVHW041348100820
586003BV00011BA/233